Architects of Little Rock

Architects of Little Rock 1833–1950

Charles Witsell and Gordon Wittenberg
With Marylyn Jackson Parins

The University of Arkansas Press
FAYETTEVILLE ◆ 2014

ISBN-10: 1-55728-662-0
ISBN-13: 978-1-55728-662-8

18 17 16 15 14 5 4 3 2 1

Text design by Ellen Beeler

⊗ The paper used in this publication meets the minimum requirements of the American National Standard for Permanence of Paper for Printed Library Materials Z39.48–1984.

Library of Congress Control Number: 2013956224

Arkansas Humanities Council

This project is supported in part by grants from the Arkansas Humanities Council, the Department of Arkansas Heritage, the Fay Jones School of Architecture at the University of Arkansas, and the Arkansas Chapter of the American Institute of Architects.

CONTENTS

ACKNOWLEDGMENTS

We are both retired architects who discovered that we share a common interest in writing about our profession; a number of conversations focused that interest on producing this book. A generous grant from the Arkansas Endowment for the Humanities funded research and photography. The Fay Jones School of Architecture sponsored the entire undertaking and assisted with the accounting and financial planning.

As authors, we are acutely aware that we are neither professional historians nor writers; we are architects. We selected Dr. Marylyn Jackson Parins, Professor of English, Emerita, at the University of Arkansas, Little Rock, to edit the very rough text for format, continuity, clarity, and, in many instances, accuracy.

Creating this new book proved to be a larger undertaking than we anticipated, involving hundreds of hours of research trying to link architects and their buildings. For whatever reason, architects seldom receive credit in the media for their work.

It is inevitable that, in a task such as this, some mistakes and inconsistencies will remain. Please call these to our attention so some future edition may be corrected.

We are grateful to the Arkansas Endowment for the Humanities and to the Fay Jones School of Architecture at the University of Arkansas, Fayetteville, for the generous support that has made this book possible. In addition, we wish to thank the following people and institutions for valuable assistance: the Arkansas Historic Preservation Program, Missy McSwain, Ralph Wilcox, Rachel Silva, and Van Zbinden; the Arkansas History Commission and its staff; the Arkansas Studies Institute, the Butler Center, David Strickland, Brian Robertson, Stephanie Bayless, and Rod Lorenzen; UALR Special Collection Archives at the A.S.I., Linda Pine, archivist, and Kaye Lundgren, archival assistant; University of Arkansas for Medical Sciences Campus, Special Collections, Amanda Saar, director; University of Arkansas Libraries, Tom Dillard, former director of Special Collections, and Geoffrey Stark, Reading Room supervisor; Trey Berry, PhD, advisor; Bill Worthen, director of the Historic Arkansas Museum, and Ethel Goodstein-Murphree, PhD, associate dean of the Fay Jones School of Architecture, University of Arkansas, Fayetteville (both were early readers of the manuscript); Old State House Museum, Bill Gatewood, director, Joe Ellen Maack, curator, and Gail Stevens, curator; Historic Arkansas Museum, Swannee Bennett, chief curator and assistant director; MacArthur Museum of Military History, Stephan McAteer; Arkansas State Capitol, David Ware, capitol historian, and Jen Hughes, archives and exhibits specialist; Fay Jones School of Architecture at the University of Arkansas, Fayetteville, Jeff Shannon, dean, and Marianne Hill, CPA, CIA, financial officer; Mosaic Templars Cultural Center, Bryan McDade, curator of collections, and Heather Zbinden, former assistant director and chief curator; Southern Reprographics, Philip McCorley and Dana Brown; Roselawn Cemetery, Bob Pointer, manager; Ed and Laura Sergeant (for sharing their Frank Gibb research); Witsell Evans Rasco, Architects (for supporting the project), and Brittany Dyer (for tireless word processing); Jim Pfeifer (for access to the Howard Eichenbaum interview); The University of Arkansas Press at the University of Arkansas, Fayetteville, Larry Malley, former director and editor, and Brian King, managing editor; St. Vincent Health

System, Jamie H. Jones, chief of guest relations; Wittenberg, Delony, and Davidson, Architects (for supporting the project), and Jennefer Kimberling (for typing and processing); Baptist Health Center, Cindy Lewis, manager of strategic development; KTHV, David Craft, vice president/marketing and promotions; Chris Allen (for the Bill Allen photo); the Mark Wellborn Family Collection; the Peggy Brueggeman Family Collection; Joanne Riddick (for information about Hunter McDonnell, architect-in-chief of the Donaghey Building); Ellen Stern, granddaughter of Gene Stern, along with family members Julia Hart, Nancy Hart, Ellen Scheengold, and Rebecca Kilmer; Wilson Stiles (for sharing his P. C. Spaulding material); Carl Miller Jr. (for sharing his historic Arkansas collection); Allan Brown (for sharing his early architects research); the Arkansas Chapter, American Institute of Architects; and Mary Kwas (for early architects information).

Architects of Little Rock

INTRODUCTION

Little Rock as a city of today is also the city of a hundred years and more ago. Nowhere is this more obvious than in its architecture. But of the early architects, especially those men who practiced in the nineteenth century (and they were all men at that time), not much is known about which architect designed which building. In addition, although buildings like the Old State House or the Tower Building of the US Arsenal in MacArthur Park are exceptions, most of the older nineteenth-century landmarks are gone and cannot be retrieved.

The short biographies in this book are about some of the architects who worked in Little Rock over the period 1833 to 1950, a span of approximately 120 years; it is hoped that these biographical sketches will provide a better understanding of the visible city that was created during those years. Through their various relationships with engineers, contractors, and clients, these architects have indelibly shaped the face of our city.

The chapter headings in this book contain both individual names and the titles of architectural firms; generally, the title reflects the focus of the chapter, either on the individual or on the work of the firm. In some cases we do not have enough information to discuss individuals at any length and must deal mostly with the attributed works. In other cases, we do have ample biographical information, but wish to emphasize the firm's contribution. Where we have named individuals, after the very early years, it is because either the individual worked with a number of firms or we wished to stress the individual achievement or both. In two cases, buildings supply the chapter title; with the Tower Building at the US Arsenal, we were not able to identify an individual architect, and with the Arkansas State Capitol, both George Mann and Cass Gilbert were involved separately and at length. In fact, Cass Gilbert has a chapter in this book only in order to conclude the story of Arkansas's most important building.

In recent years, several books featuring Little Rock buildings in photographs or postcards have been published. The focus of our book, however, is to feature the designers of the buildings. During the time period specified, there were more than one hundred Little Rock residents who called themselves architects. When generations of architects have touched the same city, a remarkable layering of human presence is achieved that makes a city unique. A number of our older buildings have survived, although a great many are gone, some needlessly lost. In coming years, new buildings will be built in the context of the old, and some old buildings will be restored. There are opportunities, when architects, developers, and laymen are joined in common purpose, to demonstrate that old and new can exist harmoniously.

Our hope is that this book will bring much-deserved attention to the many architects who gave the city of Little Rock its unique group of buildings and encourage appreciation of the fine historic buildings remaining to us. One of our lesser goals has been to identify every person who practiced architecture in Little Rock during the period 1833 to 1950. While we have no doubt missed some, our list now has 107 people. This master list can be found in appendix 1. To compile it, we used the Little Rock city directories, which were enormously helpful. These remarkable books provide the date each architect started practicing in Little Rock. However, as far as we can tell, the directories listed only white men.

Of course, not all of the architects in Little Rock were white and male. Our search for African American architects during the period prior to 1950 was helped enormously by two men, both among the first to undertake research on African American architects, one with a broad national scope, the other Arkansas oriented.

The first was Dreck Spurlock Wilson, who edited *African American Architects: A Biographical Dictionary, 1865–1945*, published in 2004. It features biographies of three African American architects with Arkansas connections. The other was Kwendeche, who in 2007 did some of the inaugural research for a seminar on African American topics, his focus being African American architects in Arkansas. He was assisted in this research by Constance Sarto, the first executive director of the Mosaic Templars Cultural Center. Kwendeche focused on six people; one did not fit into the time frame, and none of the other five, as it happened, fit the other criteria we had established for this book. Those criteria included having lived in Little Rock, having done architectural work in Little Rock, and, as noted below, having done these things between 1833 and 1950. However, although their number was small, the fact of their existence before 1950 was important, and we would like to detail briefly some of the contributions of these five.

Henry James Price was born in 1858 in Meridian, Mississippi. His fame in Arkansas is based upon his design of the one-thousand-seat Centennial Baptist Church in Helena, which was completed in 1905 (and which still stands). He apparently lived briefly in Helena before moving to Gary, Indiana, where he died in 1930. According to Dreck Wilson, in *African American Architects*, Centennial Baptist Church is the "only African American church in Arkansas designed by an African American architect and built by African Americans for an African American congregation."

W. T. Bailey, born in 1882 in Illinois, graduated from the University of Illinois in the architectural program. In 1905, he became head of the Architectural Department of the Tuskegee Institute. In 1916, he established an architectural practice in Memphis and later moved to Chicago. He designed a number of buildings in Little Rock and elsewhere in Arkansas, perhaps most notably the Mosaic State Templars Building in Little Rock (906 Broadway) in 1922. From the documentation of his career, it is clear that Bailey was a talented and prolific architect; there is no indication, however, that he ever lived in Arkansas.

Anthony N. Johns Jr., elected a fellow in the American Institute of Architects, had a successful practice in Washington, D.C., and in Maryland. For twenty years he was director of the Institute of Architecture and Planning at Morgan State University in Baltimore. His Arkansas connection is that he was born in Texarkana, but he never lived in Little Rock or did architectural work in that city.

O'Dell Lamb was born in Drew County. After service in World War II, he studied architecture at the Tuskegee Institute, graduating in 1949. He was a successful design-build contractor in Little Rock, although as his graduation date makes clear, he was just beginning a career as our book ends. Lamb is still living.

Helen Eugenia Parker, born in 1909 in Pine Bluff, Arkansas, appears to have studied architecture at Howard University; she did live in Little Rock, but her career in this city centered around teaching mathematics and serving as a librarian. Sometime before 1930 she moved to Detroit, where she worked as a draftswoman for two registered architects. As an African American and a woman, Parker faced numerous obstacles. She died sometime after 1940.

Parker reminds us of the other missing element in appendix 1: women. As will be seen, Mary Pipkin and Margaret Erhart are the only two women we have found who worked in architectural offices doing what can only be assumed was architectural work related to their training.

Why did we begin in 1833 and stop at 1950? The earliest architect we could identify was Gideon Shryock, who sent the plans for the Old State House in 1833 and sent his assistant to live in Little Rock. 1950 stands at a time of transition. World War II was over and those in the military were going back into private practice. The economy was changing from a war footing and construction was picking up. Finally, traditional architecture was changing; modern international styles began to carry more weight. While the 1950s and 1960s were exciting times for architects, our continuing to careers that peaked much after 1950 would have reduced the space available for the earlier historic period that we wished to emphasize. However, 1950 provides a convenient starting point for some future volume, which would allow the highlighting of well-known architects whose influential practices just missed the cutoff date for this volume.

The buildings built from the plans prepared by the architects included in this book were of various styles reflected throughout the country. For example, buildings of the 1830s through the 1860s reflected Greek Revival influences, and architects such as Shryock stand in this tradition. In the 1870s, we see immigrant Thomas Harding I designing the Gothic Revival St. Andrew's Cathedral.

We also see the influence of architecture guidebooks. These books gave their readers, whether architect, builder, or prospective client, sometimes detailed information about trends; they also laid out building technology. A good example of the use in Little Rock of such guides is *The Builder's Guide*, a collection of six books that had been owned by P. C. Spaulding, the designer of at least three Little Rock buildings. These books were apparently in the private Fletcher-Terry library, but at some point they were purchased by an antiques dealer and subsequently acquired by Little Rock architectural historian Wilson Stiles. The important point is that whether by understudy and apprenticeship, by formal education, or by books, architectural trends at the national level were reflected in Little Rock as well.

Gideon Shryock

SO FAR AS WE KNOW, Gideon Shryock never set foot in Arkansas, but he begins this book because he was the architect of the handsome Greek Revival structure now called the Old State House, begun when Arkansas was still a territory. But credit for the construction of what was planned as the new territory's capitol goes to Arkansas's first territorial governor, John Pope.

Pope began discussion of this building as early as 1829 in his first message as newly appointed governor. Pope and Ambrose Sevier, Arkansas's territorial delegate to Congress, were successful in assuring the funding of construction by a congressional grant of ten sections of land, which were to be sold to fund the proposed building. Robert Crittenden, still a young man when he became territorial secretary, had built a substantial brick house at Seventh and Scott Streets. It was perhaps too grand for a young man's budget, for he proposed that the new territory buy it from him to use as the capitol. Governor Pope, however, opposed this plan as he felt that the house was not sufficient and the location not impressive. Pope's vision for the capitol was recorded in the *Journals of the Seventh Session of the [Arkansas] General Assembly*; as he expressed it,

> The Capitol should be near and if practicable in view of the river. The state house, built with taste and excellence, near the fine river which passes this town, would command the admiration and respect of the passing stranger and have a moral and political influence on the whole community. Such a building would give an impulse to the general improvement of the country, [and] better houses would soon appear throughout the land.

After deciding on the location—Markham Street at its T-junction with Louisiana Street—Pope, who had begun his political life in Kentucky, selected Shryock, an already established architect from that state, to design the building. Pope wanted a grand building that would elevate the senses, one that would be impressive both from the river and from the town. He was convinced that Shryock could provide that design.

Gideon Shryock was born in November 1802, to Mathias and Elizabeth Gaugh Shryock in Lexington. He may well have grown up around construction; his father, Mathias, was identified in a newspaper account as a "practical builder." In 1823 Shryock moved to Philadelphia to study under William Strickland, the highly acclaimed architect of the Tennessee State Capitol. Earlier, Strickland had begun his own apprenticeship under Benjamin Henry Latrobe, working on the Landmark Bank of Pennsylvania. Shryock's architectural lineage, through Strickland to Latrobe, gives a remarkable national context to his work on the capitol.

Back in Kentucky, practicing architecture on his own by the late 1820s, Shryock had won commissions in Kentucky in the early 1830s, including the Kentucky State Capitol. When Governor Pope contacted him about designing the Arkansas building, he accepted. There is no record of his ever coming to

Little Rock; instead, it appears that he developed the design at long distance and sent George Weigart to Arkansas as on-site architect/superintendent.

Weigart died after spending less than a year in Little Rock, and the capitol was completed by various other men serving as superintendents. Only one piece of correspondence that was actually written by Shryock about the building has survived, but that one 1838 letter does demonstrate two things: first, the various parties could work together, even if by mail, and, second, Shryock was still involved in the project some five years after construction had begun.

Many carpenters or builders on the Arkansas frontier called themselves architects. In most cases, however, this did not imply any professional apprenticeship or formal education in architecture. Gideon Shryock was one of the exceptions. And the Old State House was a superior building. It was one of only two large public buildings in Little Rock constructed in the 1830s and 1840s; the other was the Tower Building at the US Arsenal, the subject of a separate section.

Kentucky architect Gideon Shryock was selected by territorial governor John Pope to design the Arkansas Capitol (now called the Old State House) on Markham Street in Little Rock. Construction began in 1833. *Courtesy of the Kentucky Historical Society.*

Arkansas Gazette masthead used from 1850 to 1854, showing the Old State House (building on far right) in the context that Governor Pope wanted, overlooking the Arkansas River. *Courtesy of the Old State House Museum Collection.*

An engraving put out by Scribner's, circa 1874, of the south facade of the Old State House. *Courtesy of the Old State House Museum Collection.*

George Weigart

THOUGHT TO BE ARKANSAS'S FIRST resident architect, George Weigart lived a regrettably brief life, dying in Little Rock in 1834, within a few months of his arrival. His life has scarcely been remarked on, except in the context of the Old State House and its principal designer, Gideon Shryock. Weigart was born around 1808, into a family of originally German stock.

Weigart came to Little Rock to be Shryock's on-site superintendent and architect for the State House. The project was over budget, and we assume that part of his role was to reduce the size and cost of the building in order to meet the budget.

After Weigart's death, his wife, America, and his attorney, Isaac Sutton, were appointed administrators of his estate. On Monday, September 8, 1834, they advertised a public auction of his personal property. A partial listing of the articles in the estate included normal items such as a clock, a watch, a dining table, a bedstead, a cow, and so on. But there were also several items specific to the profession of architect.

George Weigart, the architect sent by Gideon Shryock to modify the design and supervise the construction of the new Arkansas State Capitol in Little Rock, until his untimely death in 1834. *Courtesy of the Old State House Museum Collection.*

The administrators' advertisement of the sale of Weigart's possessions thus sheds some light on an architect's role in 1834 on the Arkansas frontier. The professional architect would be expected to have the "sett of Architect Books" as well as the "sett of Drawing Instruments," as mentioned in the document. Did he bring his "complete chest of Carpenter's tools" because he thought he might be involved in constructing the building? Perhaps so. One is tempted to infer that his work would include carpentry and construction as well as design and superintending.

Unfortunately, the advertisement did not itemize the "architect books"; a detailed list would have helped to answer the question of how much of the State House design came out of published carpenters' guides or pattern books and how much came from Shryock's and Weigart's creative minds.

An architect by profession, Weigart is thought to have worked with Shryock on the great Kentucky State Capitol. That he died before the Arkansas building was completed was a professional as well as a personal tragedy.

Although George Weigart died early and his wife did not stay in Arkansas, later generations of Weigarts lived here, including Samuel Weigart, a physician who practiced in Rector, Arkansas.

ADMINISTRATOR'S SALE.

WILL be sold at Public Auction, on *Monday, the 8th day of September next*, all the personal property of the late GEORGE WEIGART, deceased, consisting in part of the following articles—

One CLOCK, one WATCH
Dining Table, Bedstead
Feather Bed and Mattrass
Brass Andirons, sett China Ware
Sett Mantel Ornaments,
One Cow, a lot of Glass Ware, Chairs
A sett of Architect Books
A complete chest of Carpenter's tools
A sett of Drawing Instruments
A lot of Bed Clothing, &c. &c.

together with a lot of Household and Kitchen Furniture, and many other articles, too numerous to enumerate.

Terms—Sums of five dollars and under, cash—over that amount, six months credit, with approved security.

AMERICA WEIGART, *Adm'x.*
ISAAC SUTTON, *Adm'r.*

Little Rock, August 29, 1834. 21 2t

Advertisement of the administrators' sale of George Weigart's possessions at the time of his death. *From the* Arkansas Gazette, *August 29, 1834.*

Tower Building at the US Arsenal

IN 1836, THE YEAR ARKANSAS became a state, the US government authorized the construction of an arsenal at Little Rock. The initial funding was $14,000. The decision to build it came largely as the result of the citizens of Little Rock applying pressure to the governor, James Conway. Because of residents' desires for protection from what they perceived as the dangers of life on the frontier, Conway pushed hard for the facility.

The site for the arsenal was most likely selected in 1837 by Major Richard Bland Lee of the US Army. Lee had been sent to Little Rock specifically to pick the site, and he chose well, as it was on high ground and at the edge of town. However, on September 28, 1836, the editor of the *Arkansas Gazette* had reported that a site had been purchased for the US Arsenal campus by one Lieutenant F. L. Jones. It was a later *Gazette* article, on January 10, 1837, that announced that Lee, "to whom has been confided, by the Secretary of War, the duty of selecting a site," had done so.

Whatever the correct version, what later became City Park and then MacArthur Park was purchased by the government as a site for an army post. From Messieurs Hawkins, McLain, and Blodgett, the government purchased a thirty-six-acre tract that had formerly been a racetrack, for the sum of $3,600. The January 10, 1837, *Gazette* article described the tract as "high, beautiful and commanding."

Just how the US Army arranged for the design of its buildings is not clear, but Major Lee was assigned the title of superintending engineer, and he was in charge during parts of 1837, 1838, and 1839. It is probable that a superintending engineer like Lee

John Wormley Walker. The government sent Walker to Little Rock to be the master builder of the US Arsenal in 1838. *Courtesy of the MacArthur Museum of Arkansas Military History.*

would have worked with standardized plans used on several posts. The plans could be modified in the field to meet local requirements.

On May 27, 1837, the *Gazette* reported that Major Lee had begun, as superintending engineer, the construction of the Little Rock arsenal, on a scale to embrace a number of buildings, such as officers' quarters, barracks, gun sheds, and shops. The work had begun with an appropriation of only $14,000, but this amount was quickly increased to $30,000 for the original layout of buildings. The central building, now called the Tower Building, is still standing and is now the site of the MacArthur Museum of Arkansas Military History; it was constructed of native sandstone as well as locally fired brick.

Although projected construction clearly was not complete at this point, on Wednesday, June 27, 1838, the newspaper reported that one hundred tons of arms and ammunition had arrived for the arsenal on the steamboats *Elk* and *Little Rock* on "Saturday last."

Initially, Major Lee was clearly the superintendent. At some point during construction, Lieutenant J. F. Lee took over the superintendent's position. He signed the floor plan for the Tower Building. Was he the designer or was he the approving officer? An experienced builder, John Wormley Walker, was brought in as a government employee to be the master builder. Walker appears to have stayed on in Little Rock; his family is listed in city directories in later years. Major Lee was reassigned to the Subsistence Department, to be replaced by Lieutenant Lee of the Ordnance Corps.

In July of 1839, the plans for the Tower Building were submitted by a first lieutenant on ordnance duty, I. B. Magruder; the plans were said to have been designed and drawn by him. This is the closest we have come to confirming an actual designer, but it cannot be considered conclusive.

The *Arkansas Gazette* of March 1, 1841, carried a follow-up story about the Tower Building, reporting that the main building of the US Arsenal, "a building with an octagonal tower in which it is intended to install a hoisting machine," was complete, except for the installation of the hoisting machine or elevator. The *Gazette* noted that already stored in the building were twenty thousand stands of small arms "with accoutrements complete, a large store of munitions, a number of field pieces, etc."

So who was the *designer* of the Tower Building and its complex of twenty-six additional buildings? Major Lee had a large role as initiating superintendent; Walker had a construction role; Magruder is reported to have designed and drawn the plans of the Tower Building. Because it was an army project, and because the principals (except for Walker) were serving army officers, perhaps the work was more collaborative than "individual," in the way a private project would have employed individual talents and recognized them.

The arsenal was completed in 1841 and deactivated in 1890. In 1892, it was traded to the city of Little Rock for one thousand acres on the north side of the river, to be a part of Fort Logan Roots.

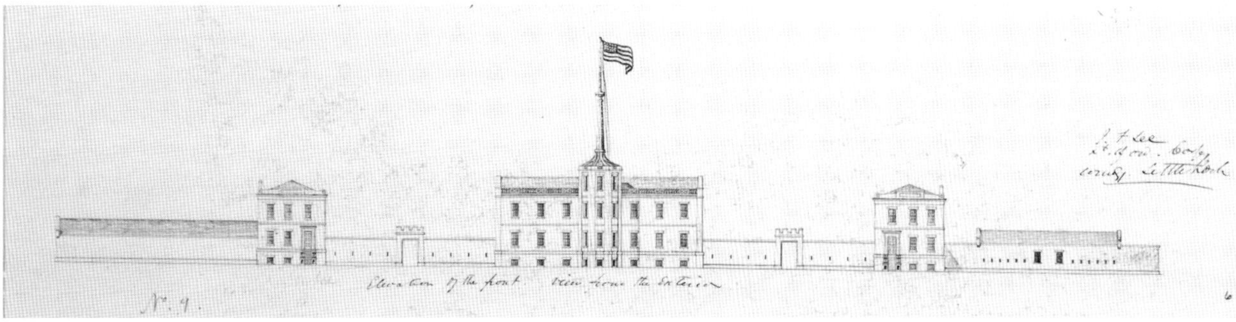

US Arsenal at MacArthur Park in Little Rock, Arkansas, circa 1840. Drawing of the front elevation as constructed by plans prepared by the US Army. *Courtesy of the MacArthur Museum of Arkansas Military History.*

US Arsenal at MacArthur Park, Little Rock, circa 1840. Period photograph of the arsenal with the Tower Building (on left) and commanding officers' house (on right). *Courtesy of the MacArthur Museum of Arkansas Military History.*

US Arsenal at MacArthur Park, Little Rock. This is an 1860s engraving of the Tower Building with a promenade of citizens. *Courtesy of the MacArthur Museum of Arkansas Military History.*

R. Larrimore

THE FIRST REFERENCE TO an architect living in Little Rock—other than George Weigart, who came to superintend the State House construction—was to one R. Larrimore. We know that he was here by October 19, 1844, as the advertisements he had purchased in the *Arkansas Banner* and the *Temperance Journal* ran on that date. The ad ran as follows:

> R. Larrimore, Architect and Undertaker, offers his services to the People of Arkansas, as being qualified for this discharge of his duty in any of the five orders of architecture. Either in designs or execution of the work. He will give drawings and estimates for either brick or framed buildings at reasonable charges, such as will suit the times.
>
> Letters addressed to R. Larrimore, to the care of the editor of the *Arkansas Banner* or *Temperance Journal*, post paid, October 19, 1844.

It appears that he lived in Little Rock for about a year. His name does not appear in the tax records for 1844 to 1847. His advertisement appeared in the *Arkansas Banner* from October 19, 1844, through October 2, 1845.

One might wonder at the use of the title "Architect and Undertaker" and assume that the word "undertaker" would indicate that managing funerals was a sideline to be pursued when the architecture business was slow. Much more likely, the designation followed the older meaning of the word, where he was agreeing to "undertake" the construction of a building or some similar task. A dictionary of the English language published in 1816 defines "undertaker" as "one who engages to build for another at a certain price."

Larrimore's reference to the "five orders of architecture" does imply that he has a certain level of professional knowledge and confidence. While, presumably, he was able to practice his profession, to date we do not know of a single Little Rock building that he designed or superintended. If he arrived in Little Rock at about the time of the first advertisement, then he arrived too late for the work on the Old State House or the State and Real Estate Bank buildings, which were the most sophisticated buildings of the mid to late 1830s.

Malacha Abbot

According to *The History of Catholicity in Arkansas*, by the Historical Commission of the Diocese of Little Rock, the architect for the first St. Andrew's Cathedral building in Little Rock was Malacha Abbot, about whom nothing else is known. In 1845, the Right Reverend Andrew Byrne, D.D., Catholic bishop of Arkansas, had purchased land on the northeast corner of Second and Center Streets for a cathedral, and Abbot is said to have designed the modest frame structure. Though modest, it was a handsome wood building, a Little Rock landmark in its time. A north wing was added to accommodate the clergy. When the new cathedral at Eighth and Louisiana Streets was built, the older structure was then used, for several years, as the temporary Pulaski County Courthouse.

Exterior photograph of St. Andrew's Cathedral at Second and Center Streets in Little Rock. It was said to have been designed by Malacha Abbot, circa 1845. *Courtesy of the Arkansas History Commission.*

P. C. Spaulding

P. C. SPAULDING AND HIS brothers illustrate the difficulty of connecting the pre–Civil War builder/architect and his work. Many of these builders and architects were considered "resident architects" because when they moved here they planned to stay, at least for some period; they moved their families here. However, despite extensive research, very few buildings of these earliest architects have been connected to specific men.

The Spaulding brothers are reflected in the 1860 Pulaski County census. P. C. was then twenty-nine years old. His brothers H. S. and W. S. were listed as carpenters. All three were born in Canada. An *Arkansas Gazette* article of February 19, 1859, relates that they had been in Little Rock for about a year, suggesting arrival in approximately 1858.

Spaulding's newspaper advertisement in the same issue read as follows: "P. C. Spaulding, Architect, Little Rock, Arkansas. Will furnish Plans, Specifications and Contracts, for Private Residences, School Houses, Churches, and County buildings throughout the state."

The 1859 article praises Spaulding's operation:

> Among the most valuable of our home improvements is the planing mill of the Spaulding Brothers. It is propelled by a fine steam engine, does the work of a hundred men, and the best part to the proprietors is that they cannot carry on their various contracts for building without its aid. This is a fact speaking as to the improvement of the city. The Messrs. Spaulding are accomplished architects and builders.

And here the story of the Spaulding brothers would have ended, but for a lucky research find. Wilson Stiles, a Little Rock architectural historian, called our attention to a millwork catalog published in Cincinnati, Ohio, in 1869. It was relatively common for millwork companies to provide cost information for the mass-produced moldings, doors, windows, mantels, and columns they produced. But the Cincinnati firm, Hinkle and Company, took an

Christ Church at Fifth and Scott Streets, Little Rock, Arkansas. Constructed circa 1850 in the Gothic Revival style, it was designed by P. C. Spaulding, Architect. *From* Hinkle and Company: New Book on Building *(Cincinnati, OH: Elm Street Publishing Company, 1869).*

additional step. They provided small engravings of each building across the country for which they had furnished materials. In the firm's 1869 catalog, entitled *Hinkle and Company: New Book on Building*, three of the Little Rock buildings pictured are attributed to Spaulding.

The first of the attributed structures is the most problematic. It is Christ Episcopal Church. S. H. Smith and Company was listed as the builder, Spaulding as the architect. Christ Church was the first Episcopal church in Arkansas. The first building was a combination of brick nave and wooden, Gothic Revival tower. The church was constructed in at least two phases. According to a history of Christ Church, the brick nave was begun around 1841, and both structures were completed by around 1850. But Spaulding's work, one would think, must have been done after 1858, when the brothers moved to Little Rock, and before 1869, when the catalog was published. So either Spaulding came earlier to Little Rock than the *Gazette* understood or there was additional architectural work on Christ Church between 1850 and 1869. Or, the Hinkle catalog was simply wrong.

The other two Spaulding structures pictured were both residences, one that of Dr. W. A. Cantrell in Little Rock. The two-story house was on Scott Street, northeast corner at Seventh Street. The other was the residence of the Honorable E. H. English of the Arkansas Supreme Court. There were two other Arkansas buildings in the catalog, though not attributed to Spaulding. One was St. John's College, designed by Adolphus Heiman, east of the US Arsenal campus, and the other was a residence in Helena.

W. A. Cantrell residence at the northeast corner of Seventh and Scott Streets in Little Rock. Constructed circa 1850 in the Italianate style, it was designed by P. C. Spaulding, Architect. *From* Hinkle and Company: New Book on Building *(Cincinnati, OH: Elm Street Publishing Company, 1869).*

Honorable E. H. English residence on Louisiana Street between Eighth and Ninth Streets in Little Rock. Constructed circa 1850 in the Italianate style, it was designed by P. C. Spaulding, Architect. *From* Hinkle and Company: New Book on Building *(Cincinnati, OH: Elm Street Publishing Company, 1869).*

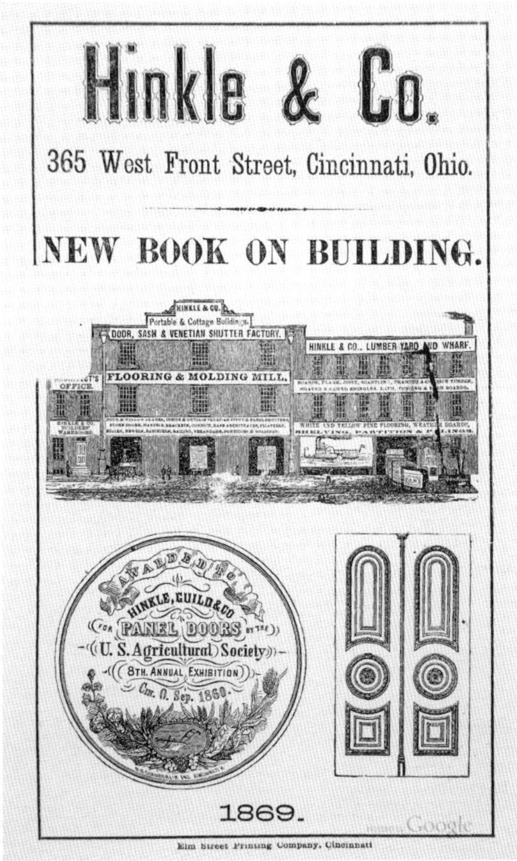

Hinkle & Co.

365 West Front Street, Cincinnati, Ohio.

NEW BOOK ON BUILDING.

1869.

Elm Street Printing Company, Cincinnati

P. C. SPAULDING,

ARCHITECT,

LITTLE ROCK, ARK.

Will furnish Plans, Specifications and Contracts, for Private Residences, School Houses, Churches AND COUNTY BUILDINGS, THROUGHOUT THE STATE.

Business card circa 1860 by P. C. Spaulding, Architect, for work "throughout the state." *Courtesy of Wilson Stiles.*

Catalog of Hinkle and Company of Cincinnati, Ohio, 1869. It contains many building examples, including three projects in Little Rock designed by P. C. Spaulding, Architect. *From* Hinkle and Company: New Book on Building *(Cincinnati, OH: Elm Street Publishing Company, 1869).*

Arnold Syberg

ARNOLD SYBERG (sometimes spelled Syburg) was born in Prussia, came to the United States, and was on the US Army rolls by 1848; apparently he was in his early twenties. He came to the United States to work in the US Geographical Survey. Syberg was appointed a captain in the army, 11th Infantry Regiment, on April 9, 1847. His name is found in the official army register for 1848. From January 1 to August 6, 1858, he was taking measurements of the Mississippi River and its levees at Cairo, Illinois.

According to his obituary in the *Arkansas Democrat* (March 8, 1900), Syberg had settled early on in Philadelphia, where he had married. He and his wife, Edith, had one son, Fred, who graduated from West Point. When Fred was working as an engineer for the Mexican government in Mexico City, he was shot and killed in an argument.

By 1860, he and his wife were living in Little Rock. In October of that year, Ralph Leland Goodrich, a young poet and teacher, arrived in Little Rock to take up a teaching post. His diary tells us that upon landing in Little Rock, he was taken to the home of Captain and Mrs. Syberg, which was to be his boarding house. His diary entry for October 18 reads in part as follows: "Saw pictures at Mrs. Syberg's. Captain Syberg was a Baron in Prussia—Baron von Arnold Syberg was his real name. . . . He was a Captain in the Mexican War and is now the Engineer of this State. Mrs. Syberg . . . is a great talker and they have some valuable books." Edith Syberg died in 1862.

When the Civil War began, Syberg joined the Confederacy. In 1864, Syberg reported for duty at Fort Towson and was placed in command by Albert Pike as the chief engineer of the District of the Indian Territory. After the war, he returned to Arkansas. In 1871, the Arkansas General Assembly passed legislation to remove "political disability" from certain people. Syberg, as a fairly recent immigrant and also a former officer in the US Army, was on that list. Incidentally, another architect on the list was Henry C. Green Sr., to be discussed in the next section.

Syberg seems to have assimilated well in his adopted home. For example, he was commissioned a colonel in the Arkansas State Militia during the Brooks-Baxter War of 1874, serving as a staff officer. Later in 1874, he was appointed state geologist for Arkansas, replacing William Hazeldine. During his tenure, Syberg filed no reports and busied himself with examining material brought to his office. However, as the *State Geological Surveys of the United States* notes, "The failure of the surveys for the years 1868–1875 to yield any geological results must be attributed to the general demoralization of the state government during the reconstruction period."

Syberg seems to have been involved more in engineering endeavors than architectural ones. Besides the engineering posts mentioned above, in 1876 he was the city engineer for Little Rock. However, we do have one example of his work as a building designer, and it is an important one—

the Temple B'nai Israel, constructed in 1871 and 1872, on Center Street between Third and Fourth Streets.

This synagogue was replaced by a new one designed by Fred Rickon and Charles Thompson in 1897, at Capitol and Broadway, which was demolished in 1972 to clear a site for the high-rise First National Bank.

Syberg died in Little Rock in 1900 and, along with his wife, is buried in Mount Holly Cemetery.

Temple B'Nai Israel on the east side of Center Street between Third and Fourth Streets, Little Rock, Arkansas. Constructed in 1871 in the Romanesque style, it was designed by Arnold Syberg, Architect. *Photograph by Charles Elias.*

Green and Edwards, Architects

THE EARLIEST LITTLE ROCK city directory was published in 1871 and contained a full-page advertisement for Green and Edwards, Architects. At that time their office was shown to be in the Wolf Block, at 109 Main Street.

Green was Henry C. Green Sr., whom the 1870 census shows to have been born in Vermont. Like Arnold Syberg, he was one of the people from whom the Arkansas legislature had removed "political disability" in 1871. His partner was John D. Edwards, who was born in Pennsylvania. The 1870 census showed Edwards to be thirty years of age; he died October 10, 1913.

By 1872, Green was advertising as Green and Son, and Edwards was practicing under his own name, with an office at #5 East Markham. In Edwards's 1872–1873 advertisement, he is practicing with or perhaps merely sharing an office with J. H. Barton. According to the thirteenth annual report of the Board of Trade (January 1, 1901), the frame building at the southeast corner of Markham and Main was used by John D. Edwards as an architect's office, and the firm of Millard and King, contractors and builders, had their office with him.

The only Little Rock house that can be connected with either of these men is the one in their advertisement, and there is no evidence either that it is an existing house or that they built it. This advertisement in the 1871 directory is the largest and most eye-catching of all the Little Rock ads. It shows a two-story, bracketed Italianate house with a three-story tower and a gallery across most of the facade. The advertisers quoted six lines of Shakespeare on house building and followed this with three paragraphs on the importance of employing an architect. The house illustrated is high style Italianate, just right for the 1850s to the 1870s.

GREEN & EDWARDS, ARCHITECTS,

WOLF BLOCK, MAIN STREET, LITTLE ROCK, ARKANSAS.

P. O. Box 419.

"When we do mean to build a domicil,
We first survey the plat, then draw the model;
And when we see the figure of the house,
We then compute the cost of the erection,
Which if we find outweighs ability,
What do we then but draw again the model."—[*Shakspeare*.

It is no uncommon thing for persons to consider plans and drawings unnecessary, and when about to build a home take upon themselves to be the architects. The consequence is that, being ignorant of the art, they get up an ill-proportioned, odd-looking building, and, when too late for remedy, they find they have paid dear for the experiment.

"In building, judicious planning may properly be computed at *more* than half the expense of a costly villa. It is an easy matter to correct whatever may be a serious error, after the plan is drawn, before the edifice is erected. But, after a building is completed, it will always be found an expensive and disagreeable operation to undo what has been done amiss, and to make a satisfactory job of a piece of work that has been designed and executed by persons having neither a practical nor theoretical knowledge of architecture."

Remember, the first thing when about to build is to obtain a plan and drawing of all the different mechanical work, and bill of items, giving the sizes, quantities and qualities of materials; with them, you will be enabled to make intelligent contracts for work and materials, and save ten times the cost of the plans, by avoiding the alterations made when working without them. Go to GREEN & EDWARDS.

Green and Edwards, Architects. Ad in the 1871 *Little Rock City Directory* includes interesting advice for good planning and design in addition to an appropriate quote from Shakespeare. It is assumed that the residence shown was a design by the firm. *Little Rock City Directory, 1871.*

Thomas Harding I

THE FIRST THOMAS HARDING in Little Rock must have been a major architectural presence during the twenty-six-year period in which he practiced. From 1869, the year of his arrival in Little Rock, to 1895, when he died, the buildings that have been identified as his designs are very impressive, especially for this post–Civil War period. He was able to win commissions and to execute designs for some of Arkansas's most important buildings of the period, whether residential, institutional, or commercial.

The census of 1870 indicates that Harding and his wife were both born in Ireland and that he was thirty-five years old, so his birth date must be 1835 or so. (It should be noted that Del Schmand, who wrote a history of the First Lutheran Church, designed by Harding, has him born in Salem, Massachusetts, and arriving in Little Rock in 1867.) Harding was the father of six children, three by his first wife and three by his second. Two of his sons followed their father into architecture. One was Rome Harding, who apparently worked at his father's firm for some years before opening an office on his own in 1897; the other was Thomas Harding Sr., who became the partner of architect Charles Thompson. (A note on identifications: There were four Thomas Hardings in succession. They are herein identified as Thomas Harding I, the subject of this sketch; his son, usually referred to as Thomas Harding Sr., the partner of Charles Thompson; Thomas Harding Jr., who was educated as an architect but practiced for only a few years with his father, choosing instead to become a professional photographer; and, finally, Thomas Harding III, a general contractor in Little Rock.)

Thomas Harding I was a prolific architect able to handle complicated building designs. He was one of Little Rock's first resident architects—that is, one who moved to Little Rock in pursuit of commissions and stayed for the remainder of his life. He apparently was able to begin designing buildings almost immediately upon arrival; perhaps some reputation had preceded him. At any rate, some of his known work dates from 1869, although he did not appear in a city directory until 1877. There he was listed as Thomas Harding, architect. But by the next year, he had gone into partnership with Alexander Bailey, his son-in-law. This arrangement lasted until 1887 when the partnership was dissolved. Harding continued in a solo practice until his death in 1895. The *Arkansas Gazette* obituary of June 21, 1895, suggests that he may have died as a result of being struck on the head by a brick at the Gans Building construction site. The Gans Building is still standing in the 200 block of Second Street.

Harding designed many of the most impressive Little Rock buildings of his time. As the *Gazette* obituary noted, "He was one of the city's most respected men and as an architect he took the highest rank." The following are some known buildings that Harding designed; there must have been many others.

NONRESIDENTIAL BUILDINGS:

The W. W. Adams block at Main and Markham, completed 1872

The Benjamin block, later called the Allis block, 1872–73

St. Andrew's Cathedral, in use by 1881, steeple completed 1887

The Board of Trade Building, completed 1887 (Harding and Bailey)

The Grand Opera House, 1872–73

Branch Normal College, 1882 (Harding and Bailey)

The German Lutheran Church, 1884 (Harding and Bailey)

RESIDENCES DESIGNED BY HARDING DURING THE PERIOD 1870 TO 1890:

The MacDonald/Wait/Newton House (now most often called the Packet House)

The James Hornibrook residence (between Arch and Broadway, not the other Hornibrook house on South Louisiana, now the Empress Bed and Breakfast)

The John M. Moore House

The Zeb Ward House

The J. H. McCarthy House

The William Durbin Blocher House

The B. D. Williams House

The Olive A. Deshon House (next door to the Villa Marre), now demolished

The Thomas Harding House

As Harding's work gained fame outside of Little Rock, he was offered other commissions; these projects included the Merchants and Planters Building, Pine Bluff; the Faulkner County Exposition Building, Conway; the Ouachita County Courthouse; and the Butler House in Austin, Texas (1887).

St. Andrew's Cathedral is a good example of Harding's talent and his skillful use of Gothic Revival style. The construction began in 1878 and the main structure was dedicated November 27, 1881. It was not until 1887 that the steeple, one of the tallest in the South, was completed. The total cost of the building was over $70,000. Built of rusticated granite ashlar from Fourche Mountain, it was reportedly the

First Lutheran Church at Eighth and Rock Streets, Little Rock. Constructed in 1886 in the Gothic Revival style, it was designed by Thomas Harding I, Architect. *From Fay Hempstead's* A Pictorial History of Arkansas *(St. Louis, MO: N. D. Thompson Publishing Co., 1890), 756.*

first Arkansas building constructed entirely of native stone.

The plan of the building reflects a typical arrangement of a nave, transepts, chancel, and apse. The structural components are very tall, and the windows are wide, providing a dramatic amount of light to the interior. Native wood was used with interior clusters of columns and pointed arches. Stained glass windows, imported from Chicago, lit the highly decorated interior surfaces. There is no evidence that the architect himself (Harding) chose paint and stencil colors, although it is reasonable to assume that he had a voice in the discussion. The combination of arches, vaults, columns, ceiling, and so on worked together to enhance the sense of the church as a house of worship. Harding's choice of Gothic Revival may seem to have been late in terms of national trends in church architecture, but for semi-remote Arkansas, probably not, and for a Roman Catholic cathedral, surely appropriate.

The Cathedral of St. Andrew at Seventh and Louisiana Streets, Little Rock. Constructed in 1881 in the Gothic Revival style, it was designed by Thomas Harding I, Architect. *From Fay Hempstead's* A Pictorial History of Arkansas *(St. Louis, MO: N. D. Thompson Publishing Co., 1890), 752.*

The imposing St. Andrew's and its architect's understanding of the needs of a liturgical church may be what caused the congregation of the German Lutheran Church to choose Harding as architect for their new church at Eighth and Rock Streets in 1884. This new church was another example of Harding's skill in Gothic Revival design; it had pointed arches, lancet windows, and ample use of stained glass. The exterior was red brick from Wrightsville in Pulaski County. Over the years the exterior surface was changed, but much of the interior remains as envisioned by Harding. The most striking features are the hammer-beam roof, the large, arched windows, and the liturgical furnishings, some of which were painted to simulate marble.

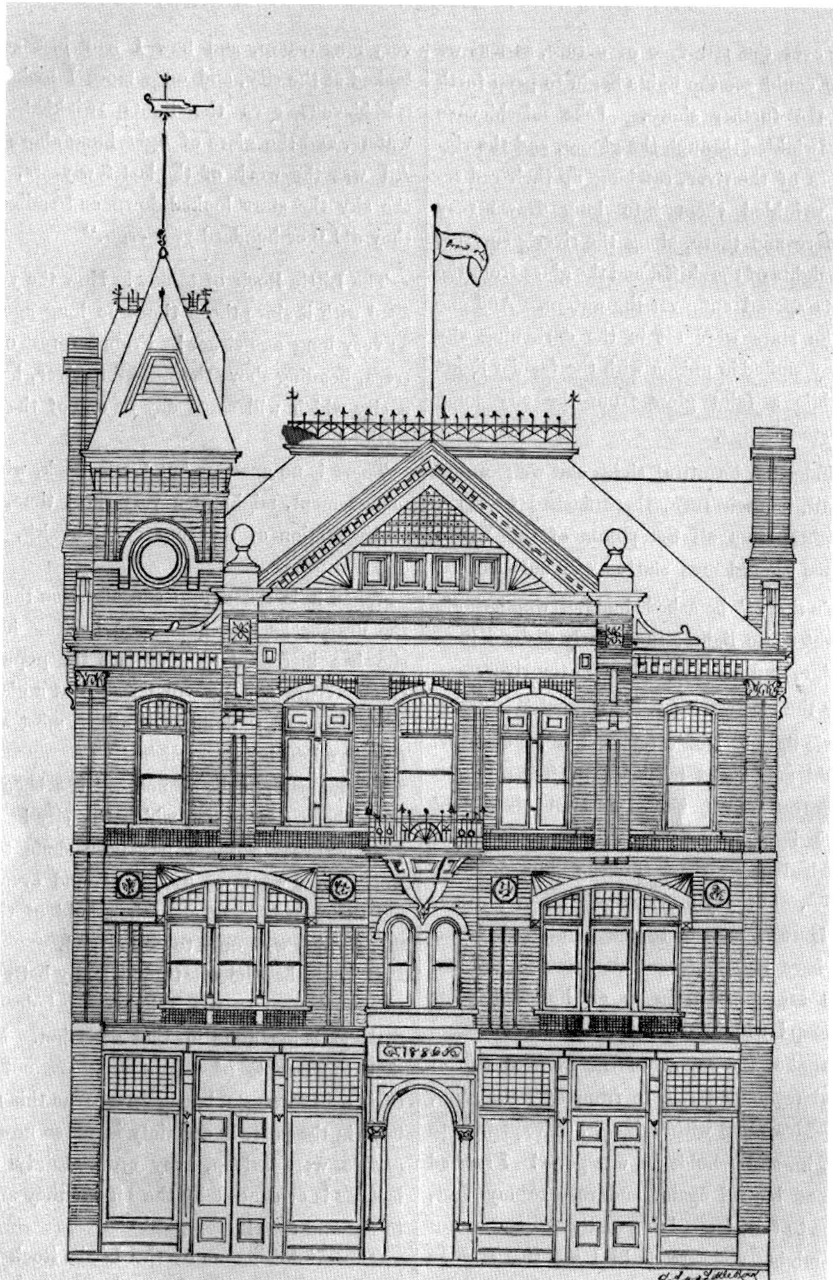

THE BOARD OF TRADE BUILDING—SOUTHEAST COR. SCOTT AND SECOND STREETS.

Drawing, assumed to be by Thomas Harding I, of the Board of Trade Building at Second and Scott Streets, Little Rock. It was constructed in 1886 in the Queen Anne style. *Courtesy of UALR Archives at the Arkansas Studies Institute.*

First National Bank, a prominent Italianate-style building at the commercial center of Little Rock at Markham and Main Streets. Constructed in 1890, it was designed by Thomas Harding I, Architect. *Charles Witsell's archives.*

Alexander M. Bailey

THOMAS HARDING'S SON-IN-LAW, Alexander Bailey, died on September 26, 1906, from electrical burns suffered while he was attempting to rescue Hazel Kirk, a neighborhood child who had become entangled in an electric wire. At the time of his death, he lived at 1616 Gaines Street.

Bailey was Harding's partner from 1878 to 1887; the firm was called Harding and Bailey. In early 1887, Bailey purchased a sawmill called the Red Mill from Butler Gibb and Company, and soon after, Harding and Bailey dissolved their partnership. Bailey would apparently concentrate more on construction materials, with the architectural design work continuing under Thomas Harding.

Bailey's branching off into the lumber business, and quite possibly his relationship as a partner to his father-in-law, help to illustrate the sometimes overlapping roles of builders and designers in the nineteenth century and beyond. An article in the *Arkansas Gazette* of March 8, 1872, makes some distinctions:

> No less than four brick [business] houses are now being built . . . which will be ornaments to the city. The most prominent of these is the large double building being constructed by Dr. W. W. Adams on the northeast corner of Main and Markham Streets. . . . J. L. Robins, who has the contract on the brickwork, estimates that it will require 400,000 bricks to build the two houses. The plans and specifications of the building or buildings were drawn up by Mr. Harding, who is superintending the construction. The estimated cost of the whole house is \$22,000 to \$25,000. When completed the corner house [store] will be occupied by McAlmont and Gibson as a drug store, and the one next to it by McGann and Bro. as a clothing house. Together they will form a very pleasing appearance and make us soon forget the disastrous fire that made their construction necessary.

A disastrous fire also figures in perhaps the last project of Alexander Bailey; this was the great fire in Hot Springs, Arkansas, in early 1905. Bailey moved for a short time to Hot Springs, where he had a number of contracts for the reconstruction of burned buildings, but it is not clear from the record whether these were architectural contracts or lumber contracts. Given his ownership of a lumber mill, the latter would seem more likely. Interestingly, Bailey was a volunteer fireman, and the pallbearers for his funeral were selected from among his fellow volunteers. Bailey's wife and two daughters, Margaret and Mary, survived him.

His obituary does not mention specific buildings on which he worked. It would be logical to assume that he was due partial credit for the buildings designed/constructed by Harding and Bailey while the firm existed, but clearly Harding was the more prominent designer.

Thomas Harding Sr.

THOMAS HARDING SR., son of the designer of the fine new St. Andrew's Cathedral, was, quite fittingly, the first person baptized there. He was born March 24, 1885, in Little Rock, and with his brother Rome got the beginnings of his architectural interest and education in his father's office.

In his early teens, in 1898, Harding began working for the very successful architect Charles Thompson. Harding's work was highly regarded and, in time, Thompson turned more and more responsibility for the architectural office over to him. Thompson offered Harding a partnership in 1916, and this arrangement lasted until 1925 (projects completed during this partnership are listed in the Charles Thompson chapter), when Harding began a solo practice that lasted until his retirement.

Thomas Harding Sr. *Courtesy of the family collection of Thomas Harding III.*

Harding lived on Broadway between Twenty-Fourth and Twenty-Fifth Streets in the house designed by his father. He and his wife, Mary Rice Harding, raised two sons, Thomas Harding Jr. and Patrick Harding. Thomas Jr. attended architecture school at Washington University in St. Louis and practiced with his father until World War II. His service in the military involved photography, and after the war he became a successful Little Rock photographer. Patrick was a real estate professional.

Thomas Sr. had an interesting hobby. Having designed the Central Fire Station, he became quite an admirer of the hard-working, brave firemen of the city and would show up at any major conflagration with a thermos of hot coffee and first-aid equipment. He was greatly appreciated and honored by the city for his "volunteer" activity.

He was an active member of the Little Rock Engineers Club, the American Institute of Architects, and St. Andrew's Cathedral parish. He died February 28, 1958, in Little Rock.

Exchange Building at Capitol Avenue and Main Street, Little Rock, Arkansas. Constructed in 1921 in the Neoclassical Revival style, it was designed by Thompson and Harding, Architects. *Courtesy of Cindy Momchilov/CameraWork.*

Federal Reserve Building at Third and Louisiana Streets, Little Rock, Arkansas, constructed in 1924. This substantial building, designed in the Neoclassical style by Thompson and Harding, Architects, now houses the eStem Public Charter School. *Courtesy of Cindy Momchilov/CameraWork.*

Winfield Methodist Church at Louisiana and Sixteenth Streets, Little Rock, Arkansas. Constructed in 1921 in the Gothic Revival style, it was designed by Thompson and Harding, Architects. *Courtesy of Cindy Momchilov/CameraWork.*

Pettefer Brothers, Architects

THE TWO BROTHERS Ambrose and Harry Pettefer first appeared in the Little Rock city directories in 1880. They had been born in England but were living in Arkansas by this time. Ambrose was the older brother, born in 1848. He and his wife, Lizzie, had a son, Ambrose, and two daughters, Laura and Lizzie. Harry was born in 1852, and there was apparently a third brother who did not join them in Little Rock. In the 1880 city directory, they are listed as "Pettefer Brothers, Architects and Builders." Their office was at 321½ Main Street, but their workshop was a separate structure at 111 East Second Street. Their advertisement goes on to say that "stair building is a specialty." By the time of the publishing of the 1886 directory, the Pettefers had expanded their services, listing themselves as "Architects, Builders, and Brick Manufacturers"; they had moved to 117 Cumberland Street.

The 1889 Sanborn Insurance Map shows the Pettefer Brothers Planing Mill at 113–115 South Cumberland. Notes on the map caution the owners that there is a hazard: "Shavings and Old Lumber Scattered Carelessly Around Yard." The planing mill was operated on steam power.

In 1890, the boiler blew. An 1891 article in *The Locomotive*, published by the Hartford Steam Boiler Inspection and Insurance Company, elaborates:

> The boiler in Pettefer Bros. planing mill, on Cumberland between Markham and Second Streets, Little Rock, Ark., exploded with terrific force on February 10th, about 9:30 o'clock. The boiler house was completely wrecked, the neighborhood receiving a shower of bricks that broke hundreds of panes of window glass. Several bricks were hurled through a front window of the evening *Democrat's* office, two blocks distance from the scene of the disaster. Parts of the boiler were hurled five blocks away from the mill, a portion of the iron landing upon the roof of Hotel Baker, 200 yards from the wreck, and many of the bricks passing through the rear windows of the hotel. Remarkably no one was injured in the accident. The damage to the mill and surrounding property is estimated at $10,000. "The sudden thawing of the pump, which the engineer believed was in working order," says the newspaper account, is said to have caused the accident. If this is the fact, it would be well to keep the pump in a freezing mixture hereafter.

Research thus far has identified only a few buildings in which the brothers appear to have had any significant design hand. The most prominent was Trinity Episcopal Cathedral, constructed in three phases between 1884 and 1891. Several phases of construction were necessary for the expansive cathedral building because fundraising for the project by Bishop Henry Pierce and others, though continuous, took place over time. Pierce's diary indicates that his son, Wallace Pierce, was the principal designer of the cathedral, working, of course, with his father, the bishop. According to his sister, Wallace

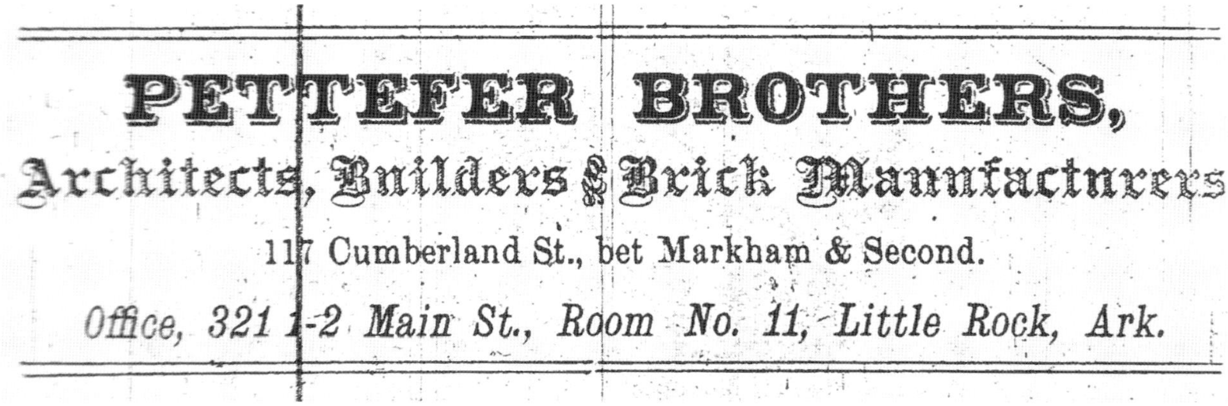
PETTEFER BROTHERS,

Architects, Builders & Brick Manufacturers

117 Cumberland St., bet Markham & Second.

Office, 321 1-2 Main St., Room No. 11, Little Rock, Ark.

Pettefer Brothers ad in the 1881 Little Rock City Directory. *Little Rock City Directory, 1881.*

Harry Pettefer Cottage at 105 East Twenty-Forth Street, Little Rock, Arkansas. It was designed and constructed by Harry Pettefer in 1888 in the Eastlake style. *Photograph by Greg Hursley.*

studied for the ministry, first at Sewanee, in Tennessee, and then at the General Theological Seminary in New York. She wrote that he then "trained as an architect" but, unfortunately, did not elaborate. Apparently, Wallace moved to Little Rock in 1883 to work on the cathedral.

We can only surmise the comparative design roles of the Pierces and the Pettefers. While Bishop Pierce was the final authority, Wallace Pierce seems to have been an inexperienced designer. The Pettefers, however, brought to the mix the practicality of years of building experience and must have generated many small—or even large—design decisions. Both the design and the construction of the cathedral appear to have been accomplished amicably among the parties, as both of the Pettefers joined the new Trinity Episcopal Cathedral parish.

It is difficult to label the Pettefers as architects more than builders. If their city directory advertisements accurately described their actual practices, they were architects and builders and, later, architects and builders and brick manufacturers. Their earliest ad noted that stair building was a specialty and added that they had a hundred lots for sale, so they were carpenters and real estate agents as well.

Two buildings constructed (and presumably designed) by the brothers were their own houses. Harry's house at 105 East Twenty-Fourth Street was constructed in an exuberant example of Eastlake style. Unfortunately, it has either burned or been demolished in the last few years. The other is Ambrose's house, still standing at 2216 Cumberland Street. While it was not the stylish house built by his brother, its utility has lasted through numerous decades.

Trinity Episcopal Cathedral at Seventeenth and Spring Streets, Little Rock. Constructed between 1884 and 1891 in Gothic Revival style, it was built and possibly designed by Pettefer Brothers, Architects and Builders. *From Emelou M. Hamilton's* Little Rock Photograph Album of the 1890s *(Little Rock, AR: James W. Bell, 1981), plate 53.*

The September 15, 1885, issue of the *Arkansas Gazette* listed a number of buildings under construction in Little Rock, including several being built by the Pettefers. Eleven were listed under the Pettefer name; some were small residential projects, but others were stores and warehouses. They include the John A. Pirtie residence, A. J. Kempner store, J. B. Miller cotton warehouse, Anderson Mills brick barn, Crystal Ice Factory (Argenta), an addition to Glenwood Park skating rink, and the brickwork on the Fort Steele Public School. The largest undertaking was almost certainly the Fort Steele School brickwork, a major project for any firm, especially in Little Rock in 1885. The large and imposing structure, long gone, was on the west side of State Street between Twelfth and Thirteenth Streets, near present-day Philander Smith College.

Ambrose Pettefer Cottage at 2216 Cumberland Street, Little Rock, Arkansas. Constructed around 1885, it was designed by Pettefer Brothers, Architects and Builders. *Photograph by Gordon Wittenberg.*

Benjamin J. Bartlett

BENJAMIN J. BARTLETT WAS BORN July 17, 1834, in Raymond, New Hampshire, where both his parents and his wife's grandparents lived. The earliest information about him includes his marriage to Ruth Hennonfitch; they had a daughter, Anna, and a son, Benjamin W. The latter joined his father's architectural practice for a few years.

Bartlett's early professional training was at the office of Gridley Bryant, an accomplished Boston architect. After serving in the Union army during the Civil War, he moved to Chicago, and later to Des Moines, Iowa, establishing himself with a specialty as an architect who designed churches.

Bartlett chose to relocate on a regular basis and is credited with designing buildings in Illinois, Indiana, Iowa, Wisconsin, Kansas, Nebraska, Colorado, Mississippi, and Wyoming, as well as Arkansas. His model of professional practice was that of a nomad, following the work, always seeking a new client. From his work in Little Rock, it appears that he favored Queen Anne style.

An article in the September 15, 1885, issue of the *Arkansas Gazette* may contain the first mention of Bartlett's coming to Little Rock; it announced that Bartlett's designs for the state blind asylum had been adopted and that he had moved to Little Rock with his family. The wording of the article suggests that the Arkansas School for the Blind building may have been a design competition. In any case, Bartlett did produce the work for approval prior to moving to Arkansas.

Arkansas School for the Blind at Eighteenth and Center Streets, Little Rock. Completed in 1890 in the Queen Anne style, it was designed by Benjamin Bartlett, Architect. *From Fay Hempstead's* A Pictorial History of Arkansas *(St. Louis, MO: N. D. Thompson Publishing Co., 1890), 22.*

The *Gazette* writer waxed enthusiastic on the status of architecture in the city: "During the last few years a tendency has been observed in the city to build better and handsomer buildings, both public and private. The growing demand for architectural beauty and the rapid growth of the city have attracted a number of architects and builders."

Apparently, Bartlett came to Little Rock to oversee the design and construction of the Arkansas School for the Blind at Eighteenth and Center Streets. The project attracted much attention, and early publications describe the work as a new "Queen Anne" building, though it is also described as a mixture of Italianate and Queen Anne styles. The *Arkansas Gazette* article cited above further states, "Mr. B. J. Bartlett has created quite a revolution in architecture. . . . He has introduced more modern ideas and methods. . . . His designs show much architectural beauty and prove that he is trained in every particular. . . . It is only reasonable to suppose that he will continue to grow in favor in the future."

Bartlett's Little Rock practice appears to have flourished, and besides the Arkansas School for the Blind, his firm would design the Arkansas Deaf Mute Institute, the new Second Baptist Church, the new county jail, and the new Capitol Opera House, across the street from the Old State House; there were also projects at the Arkansas Insane Asylum from 1885 to 1890. In addition, he supervised construction of the "new" Christ Episcopal Church (the Christ Church, built in the 1840s had burned, and this new structure, too, would be destroyed by fire in 1938.)

To accomplish all this work, Bartlett added young architects to his staff, and at least two of them made an enduring mark in the growing city. Besides his son, Benjamin W. Bartlett, he had hired Max Orlopp Jr. in 1885; the latter would form the partnership Orlopp and Kusener, which would design the Pulaski County Courthouse. Another hire was Charles L. Thompson, who moved to Little Rock in 1886. His work and talent so impressed Bartlett that he was made a partner in 1888, and the firm became Bartlett and Thompson. In 1890, Bartlett received a commission to design a new courthouse in Rosedale, Mississippi, and decided to move on to the new location, turning the practice over to Thompson.

Bartlett was very dedicated to his profession and spent many hours working to establish the Arkansas Society of Engineers, Architects, and Surveyors, A.S.E.A.S. This organization's goals were the professional improvement of its members, the encouragement of social intercourse among men of practical science, and the advancement of engineering, architecture, and surveying. His efforts were successful, and A.S.E.A.S. was formed in 1887 but appears to have lasted for only three years, its decline perhaps coinciding with Bartlett's departure.

One of his major accomplishments was to suggest that architects play an important role in determining proper methods for adequate sanitary systems, waste disposal, and the growing problem of storm and wastewater disposal. He died in Chicago from a heart attack in 1894.

On September 18, 1915, the *Arkansas Gazette* carried the obituary of Benjamin W. Bartlett, the son of Benjamin J. The advertisement in the *Gazette* back in July of 1885, at the time of the family's arrival, had listed the company as "B. J. Bartlett and Son, Architects and Superintendents of Building." However, the later obituary writer did not list any of the son's buildings, except to give him some credit for working with his father on various projects. Although he seems to have been living in Little Rock, there is no explanation as to what the younger Bartlett did after his father moved to Mississippi.

Benjamin J. Bartlett lived in Little Rock for only about four years, but in that short period his influence colored both the style of the larger buildings of the day and practical engineering features, such as sanitary engineering. Because of his frequent relocations, he no doubt helped to spread the popularity for Late Victorian Queen Anne style, but the new building he saw in the cities he visited equipped him with a more observant eye, from which his work in Little Rock benefited.

Arkansas Deaf Mute Institute on West Markham Street, Little Rock. Constructed in 1886 in the Queen Anne style, it was designed by Benjamin Bartlett, Architect. *From Fay Hempstead's* A Pictorial History of Arkansas *(St. Louis, MO: N. D. Thompson Publishing Co., 1890), 719.*

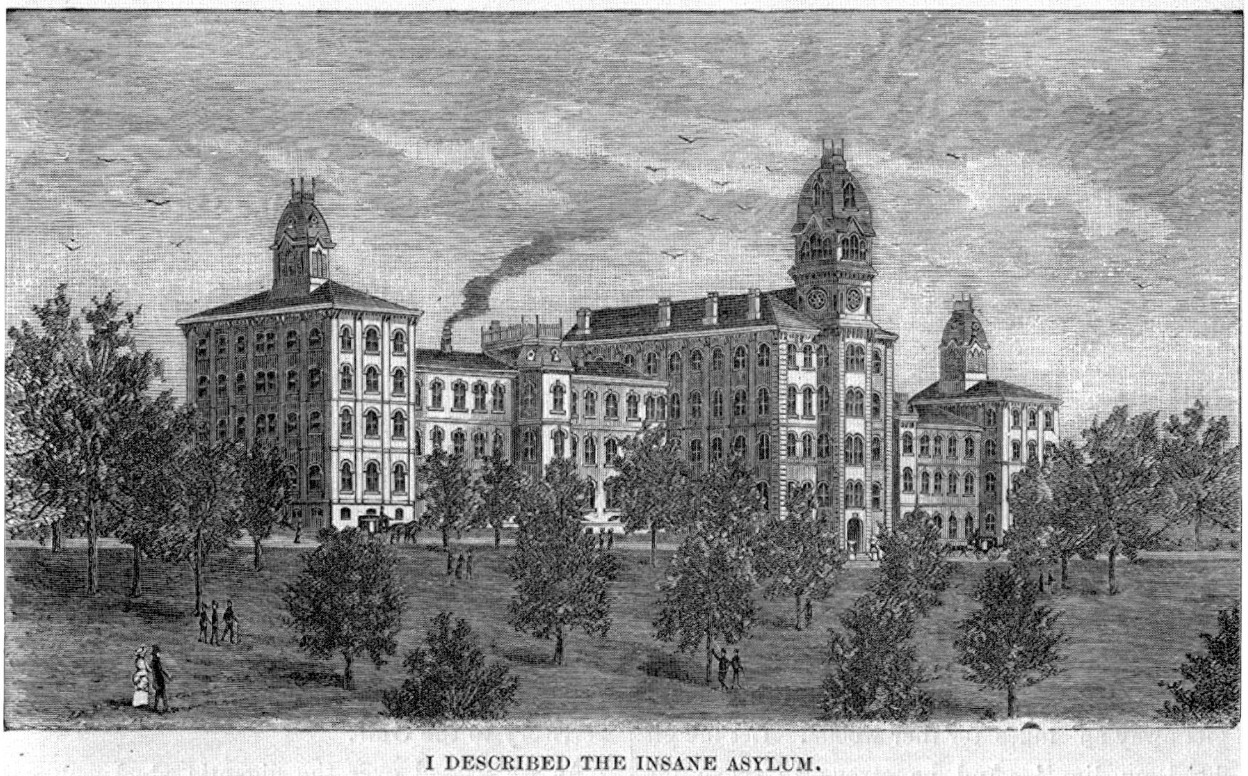

I DESCRIBED THE INSANE ASYLUM.

Arkansas Insane Asylum on West Markham Street, Little Rock. Constructed in 1885 in a Monumental Italianate style, it was designed by Benjamin Bartlett, Architect. *Courtesy of the UALR Archives at the Arkansas Studies Institute.*

Rickon and Harris, Architects

THE RELATIONSHIP BETWEEN engineers and architects can be better understood by examining the range of professional services offered by the 1886 *Little Rock City Directory* advertisement for the Rickon and Harris firm: "Civil and Mining Engineers and Architects, with specialties: Land surveys, timber inspections, topographical surveys, plans, designs, details and specifications for residences, stores, warehouses, mills, public edifices, etc., etc., railroad engineering, heavy roofs and bridges, qualitative analysis of materials." The majority of the professional services listed here fall within engineering disciplines.

Fred Rickon was born and raised in Canada; and Elmo Harris, in South Carolina. It appears that Harris left the partnership after only a very few years, and he disappeared from Little Rock records. But Fred Rickon formed a new partnership in 1891, this time with Charles L. Thompson. The catalyst for organizing this new firm was a statewide competition for the design of a monumental Little Rock exposition hall. Unfortunately, it was never built. In spite of that disappointment, the two men appear to have had a successful practice, for by the beginning of 1895, their brochure to their clients and prospective clients listed approximately forty-five projects, half in Little Rock and half out in the state (plus one in Louisiana). Among them were the Hemingway and Ragland Houses in Little Rock and the Rector Bathhouse in Hot Springs. While many of their early projects were residences, a number were more substantial. There were several college and school buildings, banks, commercial structures, a hotel, and a courthouse. Their largest project was the splendid Temple B'nai Israel, built in 1897 on the northeast corner of Capitol and Broadway.

Though Rickon left the partnership after 1897, he remained active in the community, where he served as city engineer and as first president of the Arkansas Society of Engineers, Architects, and Surveyors.

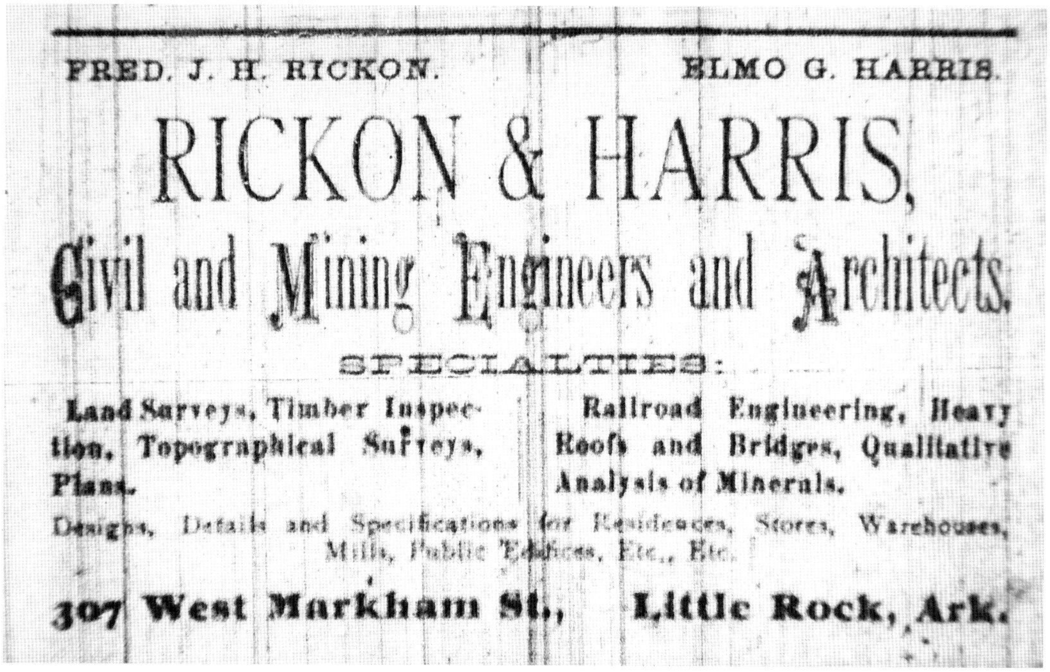

FRED. J. H. RICKON. ELMO G. HARRIS.

RICKON & HARRIS,

Civil and Mining Engineers and Architects.

SPECIALTIES:

Land Surveys, Timber Inspection, Topographical Surveys, Plans.

Railroad Engineering, Heavy Roofs and Bridges, Qualitative Analysis of Minerals.

Designs, Details and Specifications for Residences, Stores, Warehouses, Mills, Public Edifices, Etc., Etc.

307 West Markham St., Little Rock, Ark.

Rickon and Harris, Architects, ad in the 1886 *Little Rock City Directory. Little Rock City Directory, 1886.*

Drawing of the Little Rock Exposition Building (never built), on the cover of an 1891 New Year's greeting by Rickon and Thompson, Architects. *Charles Witsell's archives, from Elizabeth J. Duncan.*

Frank W. Gibb

FRANK W. GIBB WAS BORN in Rutland, Vermont, February 24, 1861, and died at home at 1609 Arch Street in Little Rock on November 4, 1932. His parents were Edward Wooster and Isabella Emerson Gibb. The family moved to Little Rock in 1871 from Chicago after the great fire there destroyed Edward Gibb's carriage furnishings business. At the time, Frank was ten years old.

Frank Gibb was educated in Chicago and Little Rock schools and graduated from the Missouri School of Mines at Rolla in 1881. After college, Frank returned to Little Rock and, according to ads in the Little Rock city directories of the time, he was engaged as an analytical chemist and assayer as well as a consultant in mining and minerals. He was listed as a member of the American Institute of Mining Engineers.

Little Rock High School at Fifteenth and Scott Streets. Constructed in 1904 in the Neoclassical style, it was designed by Frank Gibb, Architect. *Courtesy of Janet Warlick/Camerawork.*

On September 16, 1887, Gibb married Mary W. Newton at the bride's home on Lincoln Avenue, after which, the *Arkansas Gazette* reported, they took the 7:00 p.m. Cannonball Train to carry them away on their honeymoon. They eventually had three children.

From 1881 to 1887, Gibb's father, in connection with his lumber and building materials business, had purchased land in what is now part of the Governor's Mansion neighborhood of Little Rock. Included were tracts along Broadway to Gaines Street and Eighteenth to Twentieth Streets for development of rental houses, speculative houses, and residential lots.

This period is apparently when Gibb's career as an architect began, designing houses for his father's development and houses for people who bought lots. And it is a very identifiable group of houses; as one architect has noted, all these houses share certain features, most notably, round or round-headed windows. Massing and certain other details, particularly the treatment of gables, are also similar.

First United Methodist Church at Eighth and Center Streets, Little Rock, Arkansas. Constructed in 1900 in the Romanesque Revival style, it was designed by Frank Gibb, Architect. *Charles Witsell's archives.*

From this beginning, Frank Gibb would develop a distinguished architectural practice in Little Rock and in Arkansas. His skill in design and his engineering experience in construction made an ideal fit for the practice of architecture. He was noted for his fine monumental public buildings as well as for his extensive residential work. Over the years Gibb would design public buildings, churches, hotels, office buildings, and over fifty residences. His accomplishments rank him as one of Arkansas's outstanding local architects.

His practice began in 1890 as F. W. Gibb, Architect. The *Little Rock City Directory* of 1893–94 lists a one-year partnership, Gibb and Breysacher, with Augustus L. Breysacher, but no projects can, so far, be attached to this firm. Another partnership, Mann and Gibb, appears from 1900 to 1903, this one with the famous Arkansas architect George R. Mann. This association, though, was just for a new state penitentiary; the old penitentiary was being demolished to make way for the new state capitol on its site.

In 1906, Gibb formed a partnership with Theo Sanders—Gibb and Sanders, Architects. This was a very successful partnership, and the firm designed a number of major public buildings in Little Rock and around the rest of the state. Though productive, this association, too, was short-lived, ending in 1908. From then until his death on November 4, 1932, Gibb practiced as Frank Gibb, Architect. Some of his most significant projects included the following:

The Arkansas State Building at the 1904 Louisiana Exposition in St. Louis (later moved to Fayetteville, Arkansas)
Little Rock High School (later East Side Junior High), Fourteenth and Scott Streets, 1906
First Methodist Church, Eighth and Center Streets, 1900
Addition to the Arkansas Insane Asylum, 1882
Addition to the Arkansas Deaf Mute Institute, West Markham Street

Arkansas State Building in Neoclassical style at the 1904 St. Louis World's Fair, commemorating the Louisiana Purchase. It was designed by Frank Gibb, Architect. *Charles Witsell's archives.*

YMCA Building, Fifth and Scott Streets (now the *Arkansas Democrat Gazette* Building), Gibb and Sanders, 1904
Buckstaff Bath House, Hot Springs
Country Club of Little Rock, original clubhouse
Eighteen county courthouses in Arkansas
Over fifty residences

In the 1897–98 Little Rock city directory, Gibb ran an advertisement in which he listed over fifty of his projects—some residences, some public buildings, some churches. While the list does not, of course, span his entire career, such an ad, dated, is a welcome boon to the researcher.

YMCA Building (now *Arkansas Democrat Gazette* Building) at Capitol and Scott Streets, Little Rock. Constructed in 1904 in the Colonial Revival style, it was designed by Gibb and Sanders, Architects. *Photograph by Greg Hursley.*

Orlopp and Kusener, Architects

MAXMILLIAN ORLOPP JR. WAS BORN in Brooklyn, New York, the son of Max Sr. and Harriet Orlopp, both natives of Germany. Max Sr. had arrived in New York as a political exile from Germany. In 1856, he married Harriet Hail in Cincinnati, Ohio. He was a hardware merchant, and after time spent in Cincinnati, New York, and Chicago, he came to Little Rock. The 1872 Little Rock city directory lists him as the owner of Orlopp and Company, Hardware Store.

Max Orlopp Jr., thirteen years old at the time of the move, was educated in the Little Rock public schools and was appointed to the Naval Academy at Annapolis, Maryland, on June 19, 1876. The records are confusing, but a letter from the US Navy archives division, enclosing two full-length photographs of Orlopp in uniform, refers to him as a "non-graduate—class of 1881." He spent the next few years with the US Engineers as a civil engineer specializing in railroad surveys.

Orlopp returned to Little Rock and in 1885 became a draftsman for Benjamin J. Bartlett, one of the early post–Civil War architects to come to Arkansas. As seen in an earlier section, Bartlett was very prominent and had designed large city projects like the Arkansas School for the Blind on Center Street and the Arkansas Deaf Mute Institute on West Markham. Orlopp worked for Bartlett for eleven months, then practiced alone for less than a year before forming a partnership with Casper Kusener Jr. in 1886. Orlopp is also listed in the 1887 city directory as Little Rock's city engineer.

This was another case of combining a person with education and experience in engineering with someone well-trained and talented in architecture. Orlopp and Kusener blended their particular skills in a way that developed one of the really outstanding early architectural practices in the state. Orlopp's strength initially must have been engineering, although in light of his later career, he may well have had design contributions as well; Kusener's European education had certainly included architecture.

Casper Kusener Jr. *Charles Witsell's archives.*

Maxmillian Orlopp Jr. at Annapolis. *Charles Witsell's archives.*

Casper Kusener Jr. was born in Germany, the son of Casper Sr. and Maria Schrage Kusener. The Kuseners immmigrated to the United States and eventually settled in Little Rock. Casper Jr. received a BA degree from the University of Berlin, Westphalia, and an MA from the College of Arts and Sciences in Amsterdam. There he studied under the direction of Alfred Tepe, one of the finest architects in the Netherlands.

Both young men married soon after setting up their firm, Orlopp first on November 15, 1887; his bride was Jessie Culver, daughter of John Culver, and they would have two daughters, Elizabeth and Helen. Kusener married Carolina Erbach on January 24, 1888, in Conway, Arkansas. She, too, was born in Germany; they had five children who survived to adulthood.

Orlopp and Kusener's most significant Arkansas project was perhaps the Pulaski County Courthouse. On July 5, 1886, the Pulaski County Court had voted to appropriate $60,000 to build a courthouse, and on October 25, 1886, the county clerk's records called for the submission of bids to build the structure. This would indicate that plans and specifications were already finished, a site selected, and property purchased.

The person appointed as building commissioner for the project was Max Orlopp Jr., acting for the firm. According to a study of the 1887 building's history by Witsell, Evans, and Rasco, Architects, he was "to superintend the erection [of the courthouse] and to submit plans and specifications therefore." Orlopp presented a bond of $10,000 to the court. The court then ordered that Orlopp be paid $1,000, with the qualification that "this allowance shall not preclude the Court from making any further allowance after another appropriation has been made." The project was bid and a contract with J. M. Brown for $58,975 was approved.

Another significant design and an early landmark in Little Rock was the seven-story Masonic Temple building at Fifth and Main, built between 1887 and 1889. It was the tallest commercial building in Little Rock for a number of years; only a few church steeples rose higher. Additionally important in their resume was the Pulaski County Hospital on Roosevelt Road, built in 1890, a three-story main building and one wing to cost $20,000 with provisions for another wing to cost $13,000.

A fine example of their residential work was the Hanger House, designed for Frances Hanger and her husband, Frederick, a farmer, granite quarry owner, and cotton gin owner. Ed Cromwell remembered a conversation he had in the 1950s or '60s with Kenneth Hanger, son of the original owners, in which Hanger, when asked about the architect, said (in effect), "Funny name. Something like Orlopp." This house, still standing at 1010 Scott Street, has been beautifully restored. Other Orlopp and Kusener residences in Little Rock include the elaborate Queen Anne Hornibrook House (now the Empress Bed and Breakfast) on South Louisiana, and perhaps the Gans House at Third and Chester.

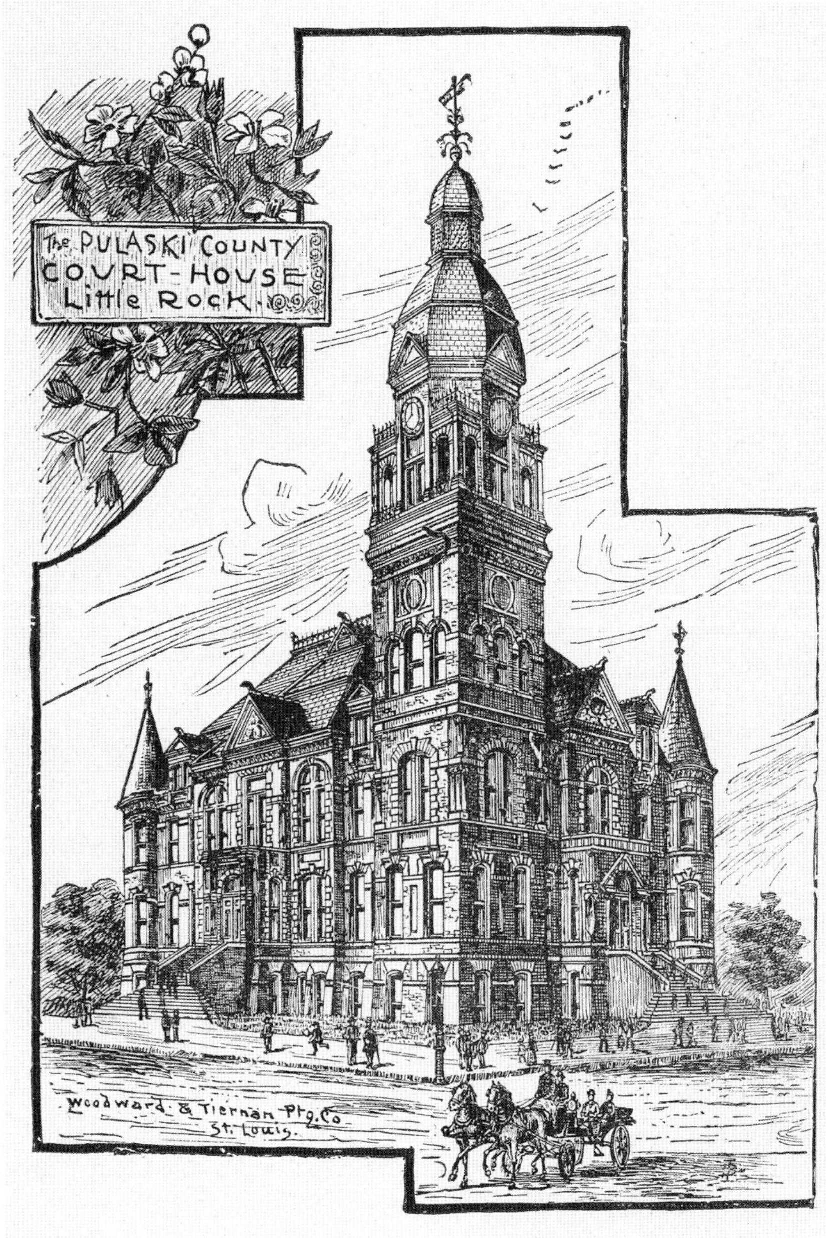

The Pulaski County Courthouse at Second and Spring Streets, Little Rock. Construction started in 1887 and finished in 1890 in the Richardson Romanesque style, designed by Orlopp and Kusener, Architects. *From Fay Hempstead's* A Pictorial History of Arkansas *(St. Louis, MO: N. D. Thompson Publishing Co., 1890), 843.*

As a contemporary observer noted in *Rambles in Manufacturing and Commercial Circles of Little Rock,*

> Many of the fine structures now beautifying our city are due to Orlopp and Kusener's acknowledged skill and professional ability. A faint idea of the extent of their business connections can be imagined when we state the plain fact that during 1887 the firm did the designing work on property to the value of over $250,000. They are thoroughly wide awake and experienced and attend to all the work of Civil Engineers, Architects and Surveyors in a very creditable, prompt, and reliable manner at very low figures for first class reliable work such as they do.

The Little Rock buildings of the partnership were designed during a short period of time—perhaps five years—and most reflect the Romanesque Revival style popularized by H. H. Richardson throughout the country. Leaving their mark on Little Rock, these ambitious young men moved on. Little Rock was, after all, a small city, and one can sense competition between architects, such as that between Bartlett's firm and Orlopp and Kusener, suggested in the *Arkansas Gazette* of January 25, 1888:

> The committee is still at work securing subscriptions to build the new athletic building [probably the Boathouse Club]. The plan for the building has not been adopted yet, but it is very likely that one of the plans made by B. J. Bartlett or Orlopp and Kusener will be selected.

The Orlopp and Kusener partnership was first listed in the city directories in 1887, called Orlopp and Kusener, Architects. Kusener lived at Fourth and Rector Streets during those years, while Orlopp was at 622 Scott Street. The 1888–89 directory labeled them as architects and superintendents. They do not appear in the directories again. In 1890, the two architects apparently opened an office in Dallas, Texas, and then moved the practice there to design the Dallas County Courthouse, at a cost of either $250,000 or $350,000 (there are conflicting records). This is the famous and still standing "Big Red," a heavy Romanesque design. Orlopp and Kusener entered design competitions for new courthouses in

The Masonic Temple at the northeast corner of Capitol Avenue and Main Street, Little Rock. Constructed in 1891–92 in the Romanesque style, as popularized by architect H. H. Richardson in the 1860s to 1880s, it was designed by Orlopp and Kusener, Architects. *From Emelou M. Hamilton's* The Little Rock Photograph Album of the 1890s *(Little Rock, AR: James W. Bell, 1981), plate 32.*

Fort Worth and San Antonio while they were working on the one in Dallas.

It is not clear exactly when each left Little Rock. According to an 1892 deposition, Kusener had been in Little Rock in 1890 but was presently working for St. Louis architect J. B. Legg, with offices in the Wainwright Building. At that point, he was thirty-one years old. The deposition related to late delivery of granite for the Bank of Commerce Building in Little Rock, a project for which he and Orlopp were architects and superintendents. It looks as if the partners went their separate ways after the completion of the Dallas County Courthouse project, with Kusener moving to St. Louis and Orlopp, at least temporarily, to New Orleans. There, Orlopp is credited with designing a criminal courts building, and he is also listed as architect for the Jasper County Courthouse in Carthage, Missouri.

Sadly, in the 1920s, Max Orlopp was declared incompetent and a guardian was appointed for him. At some point, he had returned to Dallas and died there in 1927. It is pleasant to know, though, that the firm of Orlopp and Orlopp appeared in Dallas in 1917, listed as "Architects and Engineers." Members of the firm included Donald D., Harry, Stanley, and Ward Orlopp, all sons of Max's brother, H. A. Orlopp, and all born, a descendant says, in Little Rock.

Amongst quite sparse records, Kusener was noted as architect of the Elmwood School Building in Cairo, Illinois, erected in 1908–09, and as architect of a factory in Menominee, Michigan, in 1917, at which time his address is listed in Cairo. He and his wife are buried in Conway, Arkansas.

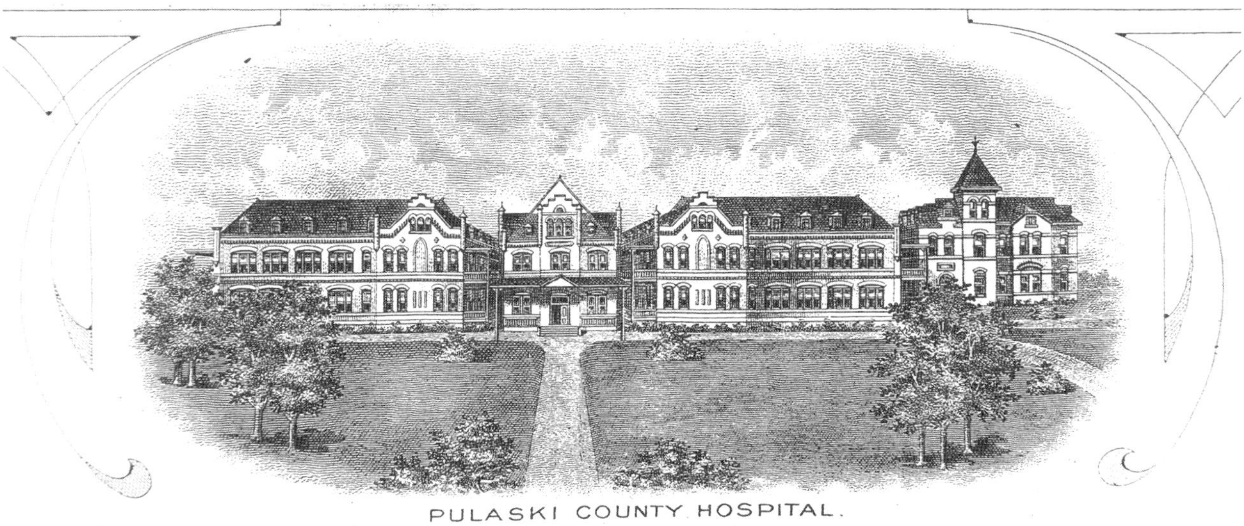

The Pulaski County Hospital on West Roosevelt Road, Little Rock, Arkansas. Constructed in 1890 in the Queen Anne style, it was designed by Orlopp and Kusener, Architects. *Charles Witsell's archives.*

Charles L. Thompson

CHARLES THOMPSON WAS a very prolific architect who created one of the most successful architectural practices in Arkansas during the late nineteenth century and the first half of the twentieth. His firm designed approximately 2,500 buildings of all sizes, and hundreds of them still stand today.

Charles Thompson was born in November of 1868 in Danville, Illinois, to James C. and Henrietta Lightner Thompson. He and his six siblings were orphaned when he was fourteen, and they moved to Indiana to live with relatives. He quit school then and went to work in a mill to help support his brothers and sisters. During extra hours, he worked for an architect named Hunt, who taught him drafting and made him aware of the possibilities of architecture as a career. In 1886, not yet eighteen, Thompson responded to an advertisement in a lumber journal and joined Benjamin Bartlett in Little Rock as a draftsman. As noted above, Bartlett had moved to Arkansas only a year earlier, attracted by the architectural opportunities stimulated by the rapid growth of the city.

Thompson had found a profession that suited him well. Two years later, at the age of nineteen, he became a partner in the firm of Bartlett and Thompson. Most of the firm's commissions were public buildings, churches, and residences.

Thompson married Lillian McGann in 1889, but she died in 1904 of tuberculosis, leaving two daughters and a son. Four years later, he married Mary Watkins, who was from one of the first families to settle in Little Rock. They also had two daughters and a son.

In 1890, Bartlett moved to Mississippi, conveying his share of the company to Thompson. From the beginning of Thompson's career, he proved himself a master at the business side of architecture, developing social and civic relationships with business leaders throughout the state. Over the next forty-eight years, Thompson developed a thriving architectural practice and designed a large number of buildings. Some of his best-known works were the Washington County Courthouse in Fayetteville (his firm designed fifteen courthouses), Little Rock City Hall, El Dorado High School, and the Peter Hotze House in Little Rock.

Thompson had a series of partners, some of whom have been discussed in previous sections. One of these was Fred Rickon, from 1891 to 1897; another was Thomas Harding Sr., who was a partner in Thompson and Harding, Architects, from 1916 to 1925. Harding had begun his training in the architectural office of his father, prominent architect Thomas Harding I, as he is referred to in these pages. Thomas Sr. started with Charles Thompson as a teenage draftsman in 1898, and as he matured, Thompson turned more and more of the responsibility for the architectural office over to him and offered a partnership in 1916. Thompson and Harding was a quite successful firm; with Thompson's established reputation and perhaps Harding's name (though Harding Sr. was well regarded in his own right), they attracted large-scale projects such as commercial structures, schools, and public buildings. Significant Little Rock projects under the Thompson and Harding name included the Federal Reserve Bank at Third and Louisiana Streets, the Exchange Bank Building at Fifth and Main Streets, the Markham Street Central Fire Station, and Winfield Methodist Church at Sixteenth and Louisiana Streets.

Another eventual partner, Frank Ginocchio, was hired as a draftsman in 1905 but left to pursue an architectural education at the University of Illinois and then to serve in World War I. He and Theodore "Theo" Sanders formed a partnership in 1919 and then merged their practices with Thompson in 1927, shortly after Harding left. The firm remained Thompson, Sanders, and Ginocchio until after Thompson's retirement.

A part of Thompson's success was his firm's ability to design buildings in popular styles even as the styles changed—to move with the times, as it were. At the beginning of his career, in the 1890s, Queen Anne style was the most popular, and his buildings of those years reflected that. Then came Romanesque Revival, Colonial Revival, Neoclassical, Tudor Revival, Prairie, Craftsman, and Art Deco styles, and Thompson, alone or with partners, adapted to each popular style. Some of the best examples of his work in varied styles are as follows:

Queen Anne, 1895, the W. E. Hemingway House, Little Rock
Romanesque, 1897, Temple B'Nai Israel, Little Rock
Colonial Revival, 1905, the J. D. Back House (one of many Colonial Revival examples)
Neoclassical, 1904, E. H. Conner House, Augusta
Neoclassical, 1904, Marlsgate, near Scott
Neoclassical, 1905, Peter Hotze House, Little Rock
Neoclassical, 1911, W. S. McClintock House, Marianna
Prairie, 1912, A. M. Keith House, Little Rock

Little Rock City Hall at Markham and Broadway Streets. Constructed in 1907 in the Neoclassical style, it was designed by Charles L. Thompson, Architect. *Charles Witsell's archives.*

Temple B'Nai Israel at Capitol Avenue and Broadway, Little Rock. Constructed in 1897 in the Romanesque Revival style, it was designed by Rickon and Thompson, Architects. *Courtesy of the Arkansas History Commission.*

The Hotze House at 1619 Louisiana Street, Little Rock, Arkansas. Constructed in 1904 in Neoclassical style, it was designed by Charles L. Thompson, Architect. *Old State House Museum Collection.*

Craftsman, 1905–07, W. E. Hemingway Barn, Fayetteville
Craftsman, 1913, W. E. Collier House, Pine Bluff
Tudor Revival, 1929, J. Merrick Moore House, Armistead Road, Little Rock
Art Deco (rare as a building style in Arkansas), 1929, Union Trust Company Building, Little Rock

Charles Thompson retired in 1938 but remained very active with various civic and outside business duties, including serving as chairman of the State Planning Commission, as president of the Little Rock Chamber of Commerce, and as a member of the Little Rock Water Commission. Like many other distinguished architects, he had served as an example and mentor to a number of younger architects. He died on December 30, 1959, at ninety-one, and was buried at Roselawn Memorial Park in Little Rock.

Charles L. Thompson in his early years in Little Rock. *Quapaw Quarter Association Records, MSS 06–15, Butler Center for Arkansas Studies, Arkansas Studies Institute.*

Charles L. Thompson. *Quapaw Quarter Association Records, MSS 06–15, Butler Center for Arkansas Studies, Arkansas Studies Institute.*

St. Edward's Catholic Church at 823 Sherman Street, Little Rock, Arkansas. Constructed in 1901 in the Gothic Revival style, it was designed by Charles L. Thompson, Architect. *Old State House Museum Collection.*

George Richard Mann

GEORGE RICHARD MANN, an architect educated at the Massachusetts Institute of Technology (M.I.T.), was hired to design the new Arkansas capitol in 1899. He moved to Little Rock and developed a highly respected practice that included many of the largest and most significant buildings constructed in the first thirty years of the twentieth century in Arkansas. When he died in 1939, he was considered by some as the "dean of Arkansas architects."

George R. Mann. *Courtesy of the Arkansas Secretary of State's Office.*

George Mann was born in Syracuse, Indiana, on July 2, 1856. He was the son of Richard F. and Elizabeth Defreese Mann. His father was in the milling business but was killed while serving in the Civil War. While growing up, when he was not in school, Mann worked on his mother's family farm. He learned mechanical drawing and received encouragement to pursue architecture from his uncle, Rollin Defreese, a furniture maker. W. H. Brown, a neighbor who was an architect, employed Mann for two years as a draftsman and urged him to apply to M.I.T., from which he graduated in 1876. He then worked a year or so for a New York firm, McKim, Mead, and White, a highly regarded and enormously successful and busy firm that became for a while the largest architectural office in the world. In an autobiographical sketch written in later years for his daughters, Mann said that he had become acquainted with Stanford White, the partner who was considered the "most adventuresome artist" of the three influential partners. The firm preferred to design Neoclassical buildings, using details that adhered to Renaissance, Georgian, and Roman sources. Mann's own building designs, often Neoclassical, were to reflect the influence of the New York firm.

In 1877 (some sources say 1879), Mann returned to the Midwest and opened an office first in Goshen, then in Minneapolis; soon, however, he moved to St. Joseph, Missouri, where the construction industry was very busy. He became a partner with Jean Jacques Eckel in the firm Eckel and Mann and designed buildings to be erected not only in

Missouri, but also in Nebraska, Iowa, Kansas, Illinois, and Texas.

In St. Joseph, Mann met and, in 1886, married Carrie L. Rock; they had three daughters: Elizabeth; Wilhelmina, who would marry J. N. Heiskell, longtime editor and president of the *Arkansas Gazette*; and Georgia, whose husband, George H. Burnett, manufactured food flavorings such as vanilla extract.

During his years in Missouri, Mann began entering regional and national design competitions; this was a way for a talented and energetic young architect to gain access to major projects. He either won or placed in several competitions, for projects including the St. Louis City Hall (with Eckel) and capitols for the states of Washington, Minnesota, and Montana.

Mann was living in St. Louis when he read that Daniel W. Jones, the governor of Arkansas, was considering a new capitol for the state. Mann visited Little Rock in 1899, and after an encouraging meeting with the governor, he sent drawings of his design for the Montana State Capitol, which had placed second in that state's design competition. The drawings were hung on the walls of the 1830s capitol, the Old State House, to generate interest in a new building. The strategy worked. The attractiveness of his drawings not only eased the passage of the bills calling for the new building but also drew attention to the architect.

In 1899, Mann was selected as architect by a seven-member commission that included future governor George W. Donaghey. Donaghey opposed Mann's selection and advocated a national design competition, but the majority of the commission voted for Mann. Shortly thereafter, Mann moved his family to Little Rock. The saga of the Arkansas State Capitol construction is detailed in the next chapter.

During the nearly ten years he worked on the Arkansas State Capitol, Mann was offered other commissions, including one for the Marion Hotel. Soon Mann had an active practice in Little Rock. Early on,

Pulaski County Courthouse Annex at Markham and Spring Streets, Little Rock, Arkansas. Constructed in 1913 in the Neoclassical style, it was designed by George R. Mann, Architect. *Charles Witsell's archives.*

State National Bank Building (Boyle Building) at Capitol Avenue and Main Street, Little Rock, Arkansas. Constructed in 1909 in the twentieth-century Commercial style, with Chicago School influence, it was designed by George R. Mann, Architect. *Charles Witsell's archives.*

he partnered for a year with Frank Gibb as Mann and Gibb, but then resumed a mostly solo practice. He designed many of the city's landmark structures during those years, including the Southern Trust Building, the Bank of Commerce, the State Bank Building (later called the Boyle Building), Blass Department Store, the Gazette Building, and the addition to the Pulaski County Courthouse.

Mann's reputation for design extended beyond central Arkansas; his major works outside this area include both the high school and the Hotel Pines in Pine Bluff; the Commerce National Bank in Shreveport; the Bentley Hotel and the city hall in Alexandria, Louisiana; and the Thompson Building as well as the Hale and the Fordyce Bathhouses in Hot Springs.

In 1913, Mann joined with Eugene J. Stern under the name Mann and Stern. By this time, he and his wife were living at 1711 Center Street. Their daughter and son-in-law, the Heiskells, lived directly behind them at 1708 Louisiana Street. That they are both houses designed by Mann is rumored in the neighborhood but has not been confirmed.

For Mann and Stern, the string of commissions for major buildings continued with the A.O.U.W. (Ancient Order of United Workmen) Building in Little Rock; the Beaumont Hotel in Beaumont, Texas; the Grimm Hotel in Texarkana, Arkansas; the Slattery Building and the Washington-Youree Hotel in Shreveport; the Union Bank and the Union County Courthouse in El Dorado; and the Arlington Hotel and the Quapaw and Ozark Bathhouses in Hot Springs. Mann described himself as the "senior architect" for Little Rock High School. Mann and Stern was one of several architectural firms associated with that building.

By 1928, the partnership with Stern had been dissolved. In the autobiographical sketch written for his daughters in 1932, Mann simply called the business relationship "unsatisfactory," though it had lasted more than a decade.

The 1929 Little Rock city directory lists George R. Mann, Wanger, and King, reflecting a new association with Harry Wanger and Milton King, both long-term employees at Mann and Stern. Harry D. Wanger was born July 24, 1892, at Moberly, Missouri, the son of Philip and Lula Wanger. Philip Wanger was a contractor, but his son chose to be associated with George Mann throughout his professional career. Writing of the termination of the Mann and Stern partnership in the short memoir he provided to his daughters, Mann said of Wanger, "I formed a new partnership with Mr. Harry Wanger, . . . who had been with us since he was a boy of 15 or 16 years," adding that "he had become a very capable architect and a first-class architectural engineer."

Because of his long relationship with Mann, Wanger was part of the design of many important Arkansas buildings, though he was not the principal designer of the firm. Like Mann, Wanger was a Mason and also a member of both the city and state chambers of commerce, as well as a Methodist. He was married in 1908 and had two children, Marguerite and Harry D. Jr. Less is known about Milton King, but in the same passage quoted above, regarding the new partnership after the separation from Stern, Mann said of King that he "was a very capable designer, office manager, and specification writer."

Among the projects of this new partnership were the Masonic Temple in Fort Smith, the rebuilding of the old Eastman Hotel in Hot Springs, North Little Rock High School, the first Worthen Bank Building at Fourth and Main Streets, and the Wallace Building.

When he died on March 20, 1939, Mann left behind a remarkable collection of beautiful buildings in the Classical, Craftsman, and Mission styles. Along with architect Charles Thompson, Mann dominated the field in Arkansas between 1900 and 1930. His major contributions were government buildings, hotels, and major business buildings, and at least part, possibly a great deal, of the Arkansas State Capitol. George Mann's professional business career was complicated both before and after his move to Little Rock. As seen in this brief biography, there were several partnerships. The following list includes some of his most important work, but only that done after his arrival in Little Rock. When one considers that Mann practiced for over twenty years before he moved to Arkansas, his body of work becomes even more impressive.

Albert Pike Memorial Temple at Second and Scott Streets, Little Rock, Arkansas. Constructed in 1924 in the Neoclassical style, it was designed by Mann and Stern, Architects. *Charles Witsell's archives.*

However, especially for the Arkansas projects when Mann and Stern were working together, the authors had difficulty determining the ones for which Mann had the greater responsibility and those for which Stern's part was the greater. The assigning of credit is made more difficult because the design and construction process can easily take more than a year; complicating the sorting-out process further is that in 1924, Mann and Stern agreed that Mann, needing a rest, would semi-retire, turning all current projects over to Stern, with Mann still receiving his share of the fees. In 1925, Stern apparently purchased Mann's interest in the firm, keeping the name. According to Mann, that proved unsatisfactory, and probably in 1927 the partnership was permanently dissolved. Therefore, we have subdivided Mann's work into four phases: Mann and Gibb; George R. Mann (mostly solo practice); Mann and Stern; and Mann, Wanger, and King. But the fact is that many of the projects were worked on by several people, and in some cases it is not possible to assign clear responsibilities.

1900–1901, MANN AND GIBB, ARCHITECTS

Four buildings at the Arkansas state penitentiary

1901–1913, GEORGE MANN, ARCHITECT

LITTLE ROCK:

Marion Hotel
Southern Trust Building
State Bank Building (Boyle Building)
Gus Blass Department Store
Auditorium at Fourteenth and Cumberland Streets
Urquart (Mann) Building
Pulaski County Courthouse Annex
Little Rock High School (joint venture, "associated" architects)
Arkansas Gazette Building

OUTSIDE LITTLE ROCK:

Pine Bluff High School and Pines Hotel, Pine Bluff, Arkansas
Commercial National Bank, Shreveport, Louisiana
Bentley Hotel and Alexandria City Hall, Alexandria, Louisiana
Thompson Building, Hot Springs, Arkansas
Fordyce and Hale Bathhouses, Hot Springs, Arkansas

1913–1924, MANN AND STERN, ARCHITECTS

LITTLE ROCK:

A.O.U.W. Building
The Albert Pike Hotel
The Albert Pike Memorial Temple
The YMCA Building at Sixth and Broadway Streets

OUTSIDE LITTLE ROCK:

Beaumont Hotel, Beaumont, Texas
The Grimm Hotel, Texarkana, Arkansas
The Slattery Building and the Washington-Youree Hotel, Shreveport, Louisiana
The Union Bank and Union County Courthouse, El Dorado, Arkansas
The Arlington Hotel and the Fordyce, Quapaw, and Ozark Bathhouses, Hot Springs, Arkansas

1928–1932, MANN, WANGER, AND KING, ARCHITECTS

Masonic Temple, Fort Smith
Rebuilding of the Eastman Hotel, Hot Springs
North Little Rock High School, North Little Rock
The Worthen Bank Building, Little Rock
The Wallace Building, Little Rock
The new state hospital, Farm Unit, Little Rock.

Arkansas State Capitol

MANN DID NOT COMPLETE the Arkansas State Capitol. Most of the exterior of the building was constructed according to his plans and under his supervision. However, the dome and the interior were constructed on substantially redesigned plans provided by New York architect Cass Gilbert.

Mann had been selected the architect for the capitol in 1899, just after the passage of Act 128, and he served in that capacity until 1909. Act 128 had created the Board of State Capitol Commissioners to act as the client. It was composed of the governor and six qualified citizens. The commissioners were to hold office until the building was completed. Of course, no one had any idea that construction would take eighteen years and extend into or through the terms of so many governors. The governors were Daniel W. Jones (1897–1901), who created the commission); Jeff Davis (1901–1907), who opposed having a new capitol; John Sebastian Little (1907), who was replaced early in his term because of illness; George W. Donaghey (1909–1913); Joseph Taylor Robinson (1913); and George Washington Hays (1913–1917), in whose term the capitol was finally completed.

When the commission selected George Mann to be the architect in 1899, it was not a unanimous vote. The governor, Daniel Jones, had wanted to select the architect by vote. Capitol commissioner Donaghey wanted a national competition. Jones won, but Donaghey did not endorse Mann. In addition, Mann negotiated a 5 percent fee, usual at the time. Both Donaghey, in his later campaign for governor, and the next governor after Jones, Jeff Davis, used "Overpaying the Architect" as a campaign issue. They brought it up over and over even though Mann defended the percentage as being the normal fee for so complex a building. Mann prevailed initially, but the issue came back to haunt him. According to Cal Ledbetter, writing in *Carpenter from Conway* (his book on Donaghey), there was ill feeling between Donaghey and Mann from the beginning.

There was also extensive argument about the cost of the building. At first, it was to cost $1,000,000. There was to be extensive use of convict labor (at one point there were two hundred convicts in use). In an effort to keep the costs down, Mann at times changed materials or altered design elements. His failure to communicate these changes to the Capitol Commission in an adequate or timely way was part of Mann's ultimate removal from the project.

The final cost of the building far exceeded $1,000,000. It was $2,205,779, more than twice the planned budget. Because there was so much controversy about the cost of the whole project, in addition to objections to Mann's 5 percent fee, there were several "outside expert" investigative panels, some of which were hostile to Mann. First, Mann had endured constant animosity and political in-fighting among governors and gubernatorial candidates; then he had to withstand the scrutiny of these experts from other places. The contractor was accused of bribery, fraud, and shoddy construction. Finally, in 1909, Mann was removed as architect of the project; it was probably not coincidental that this was the year Donaghey

Arkansas State Capitol at Capitol Avenue and Woodlane Street, Little Rock. It is Arkansas's most important Neoclassical building. As pictured here, it was originally designed by George R. Mann, Architect. *Courtesy of the Arkansas Secretary of State's Office.*

Arkansas State Capitol at Capitol Avenue and Woodlane Street, Little Rock. It was occupied in 1911. Revised (and final) design shown here is by New York architect Cass Gilbert. *Courtesy of the Arkansas Secretary of State's Office.*

became governor. Cass Gilbert was selected to complete the building, which, still unfinished, was partially occupied in 1911 and finally completed a few years later. Although Mann was not the architect after 1909, he did maintain that the interior generally followed his plan and that the dome was based on his design for the Mississippi State Capitol, which had been used with Mann's approval by Mississippi State Capitol architect Theodore Link.

Over the years of Mann's tenure as the capitol's architect, six independent studies by outside architects or engineers were carried out. These studies were authorized by various capitol commissioners or chairmen to evaluate the building's design or the general contractor's work. Mann got mixed reports, some largely positive and some not. The following is a list of those who prepared these six studies and their findings:

Theodore C. Link of St. Louis, who had designed the Mississippi State Capitol and Union Station in St. Louis. Link praised Mann's design.

Frank Day, the supervising architect of the US Treasury Department Building in Philadelphia. He congratulated the Capitol Commission for the impressive architectural effect and judicious selection of materials and good workmanship. Both Day and Link agreed that, in the name of cost control, the building was being cheapened.

Gratz Strickler, a civil engineer from St. Louis. His report was more damaging. Mann was strongly criticized for changing the specifications without thorough discussion with the commission. Mann defended his actions as necessary to keep the project in budget. Discussions of budget were a sore point. Strickler also recommended an on-site superintendent.

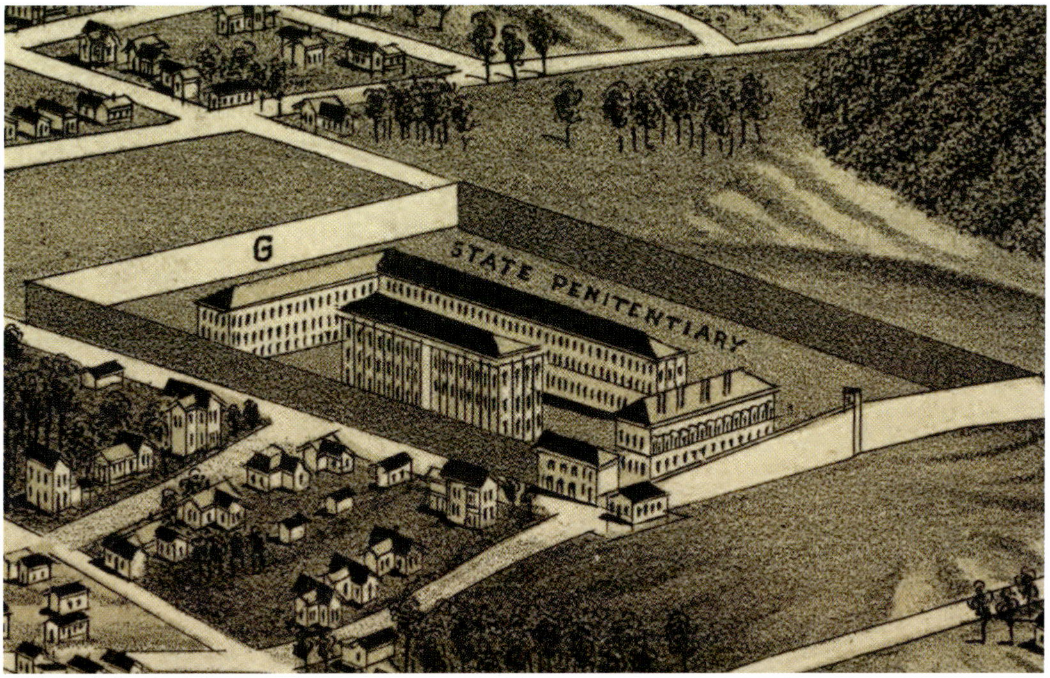

The old Arkansas State Penitentiary. The new Arkansas State Capitol was constructed on the site of the Arkansas State Penitentiary that was demolished in 1899. Detail of "Perspective map of the city of Little Rock, Ark., State Capital of Arkansas, county seat of Pulaski County. 1887. Beck and Pauli Lith. Co," col. map 46 x 77 cm. *Copyrighted for the "Gazette Printing Co.," Little Rock, Ark., LC Panoramic maps (2nd ed.), 14, Library of Congress Geography and Map Division.*

Major John Sewall, who spent two and a half days on the job in 1907. He was very critical, calling the floor strength "dangerously inadequate, only 60% as strong as it should have been." He insisted that structural elements must be replaced at a cost of approximately $175,000, a figure that Mann called absurd.

Two army engineers, recommended by the War Department, Captains Markham and Berle. Their findings were similar to those of Sewall and also damaging. Generally, these engineering reports criticized the structural design, the condition of the structure, and Mann's poor supervision of it. There were additional issues with the general contractor.

Last, there were two engineers sent in by Cass Gilbert. When these engineers completed their work, it was deemed necessary to do very significant demolition, at a cost of almost $200,000, for "defective work."

Mann was consistently criticized for poor communication with the capitol commissioners and for poor supervision and not spending enough time on the site. It is hard to sort out the rights and wrongs from politics and from Mann's burgeoning architectural career in Little Rock. However, it is fair to say that although he was severely criticized for supervision issues, the building he designed is splendid and to this day serves our state extremely well.

Arkansas State Capitol. Drawing by architect Cass Gilbert of his design, showing half of the building in finished elevation and half in cross section. *Courtesy of the Arkansas Secretary of State's Office.*

Cass Gilbert

THE ARCHITECTURAL STYLE of state capitols varies by state. That of Arkansas and a number of others follows the general form of the Capitol in Washington, D.C. They are ultimately based upon the eighteenth-century architect William Thornton's first design for the national capitol and Thomas N. Walters's addition. When Mann's proposed concepts for the building were first exhibited at the Old State House in 1899, the similarity to the national capitol was obvious and persuasive. The Arkansas State Capitol is both beautiful and substantial and presents an architectural unity and sophistication. While Cass Gilbert was not an Arkansas architect, he fulfilled a major design role in the Arkansas State Capitol, as will be seen, and thus had a hand in creating one of the state's most distinctive buildings. However, the weight of Gilbert's national reputation has distracted from the credit due George Mann for the primary design.

Once Mann was removed from the project in 1909, the new Capitol Commission, chaired by the governor, George W. Donaghey, made an offer to Cass Gilbert to finish out the architectural services for the building. Donaghey chose Gilbert very deliberately. First, his buildings reflected a sensitivity to the Beaux Arts style and his ability to design within it; second, he was highly regarded for his professional and community service. For example, he was or had been president of several organizations, such as the Architectural League of New York, the Academy of Arts and Letters, the American Institute of Architects, and the National Academy of Design. After the controversies surrounding Mann, it is easy to imagine that Donaghey wanted to select an architect whose credentials would be this easy to defend.

Gilbert was best known as an East Coast practitioner of the Beaux Arts style, but he had a number of important Midwestern buildings as well. Born in Zanesville, Ohio, he moved to St. Paul, Minnesota, and started his career working for St. Paul architect Abraham Radcliff. He studied for a year at the

New York architect Cass Gilbert. *Courtesy of the Minnesota Historical Society.*

Massachusetts Institute of Technology (M.I.T.), and then he traveled and sketched his way through Europe. When he returned, he moved to New York, where he worked for one of the leading firms in the United States—McKim, Mead, and White, in its New York and then Baltimore offices. In 1883, Gilbert returned to St. Paul and went into partnership from 1884 to 1892 with James Knox Taylor, a fellow M.I.T. classmate (and, coincidentally, one of the architects of the Little Rock Courthouse/Post Office). There he had a major client, the Northern Pacific Railroad, for whom he designed a variety of buildings.

The firm grew in popularity locally, designing houses, office buildings, warehouses, retail stores, and so on. Their buildings followed the popular styles of the day: Richardson Romanesque, Shingle style, Colonial Revival, and Renaissance Revival. But it was his winning of the competition for the Minnesota State Capitol in St. Paul that led him to national prominence. After that, several important commissions followed: the US Customs House, New York (1899–1907); the St. Louis Art Museum (1904); the St. Louis Public Library (1907–1912); the F. W. Woolworth Building in New York (1910–1913); the West Virginia Capitol; the US Treasury Annex in Washington, D.C. (1918–1919); the New York Life Insurance Company Building (1925–1928); and master plans for Oberlin College and the Universities of Minnesota and Texas. His best-known building, the US Supreme Court Building in Washington, D.C. (1928–1935), was completed after his death in 1934.

It might be said that Gilbert was a very popular designer of the "old school" at a time when designers were still influenced by the East Coast establishment's desire for academically correct designs rooted in Beaux Arts tradition. His years of greatest influence were 1900 to 1934.

Gilbert's work on the Arkansas State Capitol extended from 1909 to 1917, but most was during the two years between 1909 and 1911. On the issue of architectural fees, Gilbert had apparently quoted the same percentage as Mann, but this time Donaghey accepted the percentage without argument. In fact, Gilbert's fee was $3,500 immediately and 5 percent of the entire cost of the remainder of the work. In contrast, at the termination of Mann's services, his fee had been reduced to 4 percent.

Once the design fee was finalized, Gilbert sent two structural engineers to inspect the building. Perhaps the most critical aspect of Gilbert's engagement was the report of these two men; they recommended replacement of a number of structural components and, in particular, were concerned about the strength of the floors and the reliability of the iron and steel. As seen above, they called for significant demolition of "defective work" at a cost of nearly $200,000.

Although Mann became embroiled in political and managerial controversies that Gilbert avoided in bringing the Arkansas State Capitol project to a successful conclusion, there were many similarities between the two men. In fact, according to David Ware, the historian of the Arkansas State Capitol, it is striking how similar the two designers were. Both worked happily and authoritatively in Neoclassical and Beaux Arts styles; Gilbert may have been more versatile, but that may reflect luck of the draw in clients and their demands/desires. There are additional parallel points: both attended M.I.T., both worked at McKim, Mead, and White in New York, both had an initial partnership with a classmate, both entered competitions, including those for various state capitols, and both were able and ambitious. The fact that Gilbert and Mann placed first and second, respectively, on both the Minnesota and Montana Capitol buildings suggests that they were of roughly equal national prominence at that time. Why then did Gilbert achieve such national regard, but not Mann? Although both were gifted architects, perhaps Gilbert was better at managing the details and the salesmanship.

Theodore M. Sanders

THEODORE M. SANDERS, born in Little Rock in 1879, was the son of Fred and Fannie Sanders, who had emigrated from Germany, lived for a time in Mexico, and, improbable though it may seem, had settled in Mountain Home, Arkansas, in 1871. Theo's great-granddaughter, Laura Joseph, has outlined the family's early life in Arkansas, noting that they had attempted to farm for a living. "They lived forty miles from a railroad on poor, rocky soil." Fred built a small log house and struggled to make the ground produce, but his health failed. The starving family was rescued by a kind relative who traveled from Mississippi "by boat, train, and horseback" and helped resettle the family at Little Rock. There, Fred opened a photography business and, being fluent in four languages, served as a court reporter for foreign cases.

Theo Sanders grew up at home in Little Rock with eight brothers and sisters. He was educated in the Little Rock public schools and graduated from high school in 1897. He studied architecture at the University of Illinois and took his degree in 1902.

Union National Bank at Fourth and Louisiana Streets, Little Rock, Arkansas. Constructed in 1929 in the Art Deco style, it was designed by Thompson, Sanders, and Ginocchio, Architects. *Charles Witsell's archives.*

After college, he spent a year in Paris and studied at the prestigious École des Beaux Arts School of Design. While in Paris, and later in travel to Italy, he developed a wonderful collection of sketches and watercolors that were fine examples of his skill as an artist.

It is interesting to note that Sanders was one of the first Arkansas native-born architects to receive a formal education in architecture. Of earlier prominent architects, most were from other states and had received formal training at institutions such as Harvard, the Massachusetts Institute of Technology, and Yale, or abroad. They were often attracted to Little Rock when a large public project, like a courthouse, was to be erected. Many had designed similar projects in other states and displayed these as examples of their work. This process eventually brought a number of highly skilled and experienced architects to Arkansas, and several of them settled in Little Rock, developing large practices throughout the city and the state.

When Sanders returned to Little Rock, his first employment was with Frank Gibb, one of the leading architects of the city. Gibb soon recognized Sanders's talent and in 1906 made him a partner; the firm became Gibb and Sanders. In 1910, Sanders decided to open his own firm and began practicing as T. M. Sanders, Architect. His early solo work included schools, theaters, and residences. The Women's City Club at Fourth and Scott Streets is a fine example of his work during this period.

In 1920, Sanders and local architect Frank Ginocchio formed a partnership as Sanders and Ginocchio, Architects. This practice continued until 1927, when they joined Charles Thompson, one of Arkansas's most prominent architects, to form the firm of Thompson, Sanders, and Ginocchio, Architects. This practice became one of the largest in the state. They designed schools, courthouses, banks, office buildings, and hotels, including many of the buildings on Main Street. This grouping continued until Thompson retired in 1938. Sanders continued

Women's City Club at Fourth and Scott Streets, Little Rock, Arkansas. Constructed in 1908 in the Second Renaissance style, it was designed by Theo Sanders. *Courtesy of Janet Warlick/CameraWork.*

Ada Thompson Home at Twenty-First and Main Streets, Little Rock, Arkansas. Constructed in 1909 in the Colonial Revival style, it was designed by Sanders and Ginocchio, Architects. *Courtesy of Janet Warlick/CameraWork.*

as a partner with Ginocchio until he resumed solo practice in 1941; he continued to maintain a practice until his death in 1947.

Some of Sanders's Little Rock projects, both in solo practice and with partners, include the Union National Bank, the Ada Thompson Home, the YMCA, the Hall Building, the M. M. Cohn Department Store, the Frederica Hotel (now the Legacy), and the Cornish House.

Besides being a good architect, Theo Sanders was also a good citizen in his community and his profession. He served as president of the Arkansas Chapter of the American Institute of Architects (AIA), and because of his lifelong interest in art, he founded the Theodore M. Sanders Art Exhibit to promote art activities among young people. He was an early supporter of the public library and also taught geometry at Little Rock Junior College.

Theo Sanders as an École des Beaux Arts School of Design student in Paris circa 1903. *Quapaw Quarter Association Records, MSS 06–15, Butler Center for Arkansas Studies, Arkansas Studies Institute.*

Frank M. Blaisdell

BORN SEPTEMBER 17, 1855, in Boston, Massachusetts, Frank Blaisdell came to Little Rock from Fort Smith in 1911. He came as a civil engineer hired to lay out the Arkansas State Capitol grounds. He had studied at West Point for three years and had assisted in designing the west wing of the Army and Navy Building in Washington, D.C.

It is not clear where Blaisdell got his training in architecture. His name appeared in an ad in the 1917 edition of the Little Rock city directory: "Frank M. Blaisdell—Architect and Civil Engineer—to supply plans for public buildings, colleges, schools, churches, banks, theatres and artistic bungalows." His talent was evident in his design of Morris Hall,

Mosaic Templars Building at Ninth and Broadway Streets, Little Rock, Arkansas. Dedicated 1913, it was designed by Frank Blaisdell. *Courtesy of Arkansas State History Commission.*

St. John's Seminary, Morris Hall at 2500 North Tyler Street, Little Rock, Arkansas. Constructed in 1916 in the Collegiate Gothic style, it was designed by Frank Blaisdell. *Photograph by Gordon Wittenberg.*

the central structure of St. John's Seminary at the end of Tyler Street in the Pulaski Heights area of Little Rock. He also designed the Mosaic Templars Building at Ninth and Broadway, the headquarters of the Mosaic Templars of America, dedicated in 1913. (There were two additional Mosaic buildings during the period: first, an annex to the south of the original structure was built in 1918; then in 1921, the Mosaic State Templars Building was constructed from plans prepared by African American architect W. T. Bailey.) Blaisdell's building burned down in 2005, just as it was being renovated, but has since been reconstructed and now, with the annex, constitutes the Mosaic Templars Cultural Center, a museum of the Department of Arkansas Heritage.

Among residences, Blaisdell designed the Foster House at Twenty-Second and Gaines Streets. Other work included agricultural schools at Russellville and Jonesboro and the Administration Building at Henderson-Brown College in Arkadelphia.

Blaisdell's obituary notes that he died at his home, 5208 U Street in Pulaski Heights, after an illness of only a few hours. On November 16, 1921, he became ill while at the supper table and his condition grew rapidly worse; he was sixty-six years old.

Eugene John Stern

EUGENE JOHN STERN, called Gene by his family, was born in Budapest, Hungary, and later moved with his family to New York. His father was Jacob Stern, an insurance agent who died in 1925, and his mother was Helena Roth Stern. Their children were Howard, Olive, Virginia, Carol, and Eugene. Gene Stern was privately tutored through high school. Then he studied architecture at the Mechanics Institute in New York from 1900 to 1904. He also attended the Beaux Arts Atelier from 1904 to 1905. Stern's first professional partnership, Stern and Morris, was with Benjamin Morris in New York City; this was for only one year, 1907 to 1908. In 1908, he married Elizabeth Burger of New York City; the couple would have four children. Also in 1908, Stern relocated to North Carolina, where he was first part of Wheeler and Stern (1908–1913) with Oliver Duke Wheeler, and then the firm became Wheeler, Galliher, and Stern with the addition of C. F. Galliher.

YMCA Building at Sixth and Broadway Streets, Little Rock, Arkansas. Constructed in 1928 in the Spanish Revival style, it was designed by Eugene Stern. *Courtesy of the Historic Preservation Program.*

Albert Pike Hotel at Seventh and Scott Streets, Little Rock, Arkansas. Constructed in 1929 in the Spanish Revival style, it was designed by Mann and Stern, Architects. *Charles Witsell's archives.*

Union Life Building at 212 Center Street, Little Rock, Arkansas. Constructed from 1911 to 1917 in the Chicago style, it was designed by Mann and Stern, Architects. *Photograph by Evans Wittenberg.*

From North Carolina, Stern moved to Little Rock to join forces with George Mann in the partnership Mann and Stern. This lasted until he opened his own firm, E. J. Stern, in 1927. Young architects Howard Eichenbaum and Frank Erhart, who had been part of the Mann and Stern organization, decided to stay with Stern, while, as seen earlier, Henry Wanger and Milton King remained with Mann. Wanger had been Mann's chief draftsman for many years. George Trapp also worked for Stern at some point, as did Jack Petter, an English-born architect who had worked for William Holabird and John Wellborn Root at the distinguished firm of Holabird and Root in Chicago and spent several years in Arkansas. Erhart and Eichenbaum left the firm in the early 1930s and opened their own office.

Records now housed in the Quapaw Quarter Association archives contain a letter from Stern dated April 27, 1939; its letterhead reads as follows: "Eugene John Stern, Inc./Successor to Mann and Stern/Architect/402–6 Pyramid Building, Little Rock, Ark." Apparently, in the late 1930s and during the 1940s, Stern had an office in Kansas City as well as in Little Rock. Although he maintained his Arkansas architect's license up until at least 1951, a December 20, 1952 letter notes, "I have not been practicing in the United States for over a year." The new venue was Mexico. Stern and his first wife had divorced some years earlier, and Stern had remarried and moved to Mexico. Details of the practice in Mexico are obscure; the firm's name was "Stern de Mexico." Stern died in 1961.

A list of projects produced by the Mann and Stern partnership is listed elsewhere with George Mann's projects, and, as noted there, problems with attribution have occurred. Any list of major Little Rock buildings to which Stern contributed would include the YMCA Building at Sixth and Broadway. Much of his work was done outside Little Rock; some of those projects were the Slattery Office Building in Shreveport; the Simmons Office Building in Pine Bluff; alterations to the Bentley Office Building in Alexandria; and the El Dorado City Hall and Union County Courthouse in El Dorado.

George Trapp (left) and Eugene Stern (right). *Courtesy of Wilson Stiles.*

John Parks Almand

JOHN PARKS ALMAND worked as an architect in Arkansas for fifty years, beginning in 1912. His designs include a number of residences, hospitals, schools, businesses, and over fifty churches. Among his projects were Little Rock (Central) High School (a joint project with several other firms), First Church of Christ Scientist in Little Rock, First Presbyterian Church in Little Rock, First Methodist Church in Fordyce, Couchwood in Hot Springs, and the Medical Arts Building, also in Hot Springs.

Almand was born in Lithonia, Georgia, on May 8, 1885. He was the third of eight children of Alexander J. and Clara Bond Almand. He attended Emory College in Georgia and graduated with a BS degree in 1907. Initially interested in a career in medicine, he decided soon that his true calling was architecture and went to Columbia University in New York, where he received a Bachelor of Architecture degree in 1911. An outstanding student, Almand received scholarships during the final three years of his work at Columbia and graduated second in his class.

U. M. Rose School at Philander Smith College, Little Rock, Arkansas. Constructed in 1915 in the Colonial Revival style, it was designed by John Parks Almand, Architect. *Courtesy of Cindy Momchilov/CameraWork.*

Upon graduation, Almand spent about a year working in Havana, Cuba, for the T. L. Hudson Company. Almand was an individualist who believed that hard work was one key to success, and from early on his aim was to go into practice for himself. As a stopgap, however, hearing of a need for a designer at the Little Rock firm of Charles L. Thompson, Almand applied for the job and was accepted there. Almand worked at Charles L. Thompson and Associates from July of 1912 until December of 1915. While at the firm he worked on designs for the Central Fire Station and the Bankers Trust Building. His first commission was in May of 1915 when he designed the U. M. Rose School (now the Administration Building of Philander Smith College in Little Rock).

In January of 1916, Almand achieved his goal of opening his own architectural business. During the remainder of his career as an architect, he worked alone, with the exception of 1925, when he took on Van Valenberg as an associate, and in 1929–30, when he entered into a partnership with Elmer A. Stuck of Jonesboro. He also left private practice briefly and worked two short stints (1935–36 and 1942) on federal projects.

In early 1913, Almand had met Frances Reeve Edmonson. They were married at her home on November 4, 1914, and they had a son, Alexander James (always called A. J.), who was born on October 16, 1915. Another son, John Parks Almand Jr., was born on October 12, 1917, but died as an infant in the influenza epidemic of 1918.

It was during the 1920s that Almand's architectural practice began to grow. He designed everything from churches to hotels, office buildings, and residences. He also designed and patented a unique, mushroom-shaped service station that was built near the Arkansas State Capitol in 1923. His list of commissions (in Little Rock unless noted otherwise) include the following:

Oak Forest Methodist Church at 2415 Fair Park Boulevard, Little Rock, Arkansas. Constructed in 1949 in the Gothic Revival style, it was designed by John Parks Almand, Architect. *Courtesy of Cindy Momchilov/CameraWork.*

First Presbyterian Church. Constructed in 1921 at 800 Scott Street, Little Rock, Arkansas, in the Gothic Revival style, it was designed by John Parks Almand, Architect. *Photograph by Gordon Wittenberg.*

Arkansas Children's Hospital
Little Rock General Hospital
Administration Building at the (now) University of Central Arkansas, Conway
Couchwood, Hot Springs, the country home of Arkansas Power and Light founder Harvey Couch
Land's End Plantation, home of James R. Alexander, Scott
Bentonville High School, Bentonville
Central Baptist Church, Hot Springs
First United Methodist Church, Jonesboro
Oak Forest Methodist Church

Almand went on to design sanctuaries, chapels, education units, parsonages, and interiors at over fifty churches throughout the state, including Bald Knob, Beebe, Carlisle, Clarksville, Clinton, Conway, Crossett, DeQueen, Dumas, Fordyce, Helena, Jacksonville, Jonesboro, Lake Village, Lonoke, McGehee, Monticello, North Little Rock, Paragould, Rogers, Russellville, Searcy, Smackover, and Wynne. He also designed post offices in Fort Smith and in Columbia, Missouri, and churches in New Mexico and Louisiana.

Almand worked in a variety of architectural styles during his fifty-year career, including Craftsman, Art Deco, Colonial Revival, Tudor Revival, Gothic Revival, and California Mission. A stickler for detail, Almand recommended the finest materials to his clients. He also required high-quality workmanship from builders, and on more than one occasion is known to have told a contractor to tear out work he deemed sub-par.

In 1962, Almand suffered a stroke, which left him numb on his left side, and a second stroke occurred a year later. After this, his health progressively declined for several years and he died on March 23, 1969. Almand had been elected to the American Institute of Architects in 1921, the thirty-ninth architect registered in the state of Arkansas.

He was a member of the Rotary Club and a Scottish Rite Mason.

A devout man, Almand was a member of the First United Methodist Church in Little Rock; he taught Sunday School classes there for several years and served on the Board of Stewards for more than twenty years. He was also devoted to his family and cared for his wife, who suffered poor health over several years.

It is a testament to his abilities that Almand achieved such success and was so prolific in output while working alone for the majority of his career as an architect. He left a legacy of fine buildings throughout the state, especially the many churches that touch Arkansans in their daily lives.

As A. J. Almand said of his father, "I don't believe anyone could love architecture more than he did. He was happiest when at the board working on a design or developing a solution to a knotty problem. He would hum or whistle an original tune, and I imagine he was unaware of doing it. To design was his greatest joy."

John Parks Almand. *From the American Institute of Architects Arkansas Chapter's* Dimensions *4, no. 2 (March/April 1969).*

Wittenberg and Delony, Architects

GEORGE HYDE WITTENBERG

George Wittenberg was born in Little Rock, Arkansas, the son of Frank T. and Ruth Hyde Wittenberg, on September 5, 1892. In 1914, he married Minnie Greenfield. Their children were George Jr., Gordon, and Kathryn. Wittenberg served on the Little Rock Planning Commission, devoting his time to help with the orderly planning of the growth of the city as it became a large metropolitan area.

One of Wittenberg's proudest accomplishments was the success of his years of work to develop the Arkansas Architectural Act, passed by the state legislature in 1941. Before that time, there was no licensing, and no qualifications were required to practice architecture in Arkansas, although doctors, lawyers, and most other professionals were required to be licensed. For many years, this was not a major problem. But as technology advanced and plumbing, sanitary sewers, electricity, telephones, central heating and air-conditioning, and the use of steel and concrete developed, the need to have carefully trained and experienced architects became imperative to safeguard life, health, and property.

Wittenberg felt it was extremely important that the practice of architecture in the state be regulated. After the act was passed, he was appointed the first president of the Arkansas Architects Licensing Board, and he was issued license #1. Wittenberg died December 29, 1953.

LAWSON L. DELONY

Like George Wittenberg, Lawson Delony was also born in Little Rock, though a bit earlier, on March 4, 1890. His parents were W. L. and Cypert Delony. In 1920, Lawson Delony married Joyce Manning; their children were Irene Joyce and Lawson L. Jr.

Delony served his profession and community in many ways: he was president of the Arkansas chapter

Little Rock Central High School at 1500 S. Park Street. Constructed in 1927 in the Collegiate Gothic style and hailed as the most beautiful high school in America, it was designed by Mann and Stern, Architects; John Parks Almand, Architect; and Wittenberg and Delony, Architects. *Courtesy of Janet Warlick/CameraWork.*

of the American Institute of Architects, a vestry member at Trinity Episcopal Cathedral, president of Lakeside Country Club, director of the Florence Crittenden Home, president of Pin Oak Duck Club, and a member of Trinity Masonic Lodge 694, the Arkansas Consistory, and Scimitar Shrine Temple.

One of the activities he considered most important was his membership on the Little Rock Waterworks Commission, where he served continuously from 1949 to 1972. He felt that the commission's greatest accomplishment during that time was the creation of Lake Maumelle. He died November 20, 1976.

WITTENBERG AND DELONY, ARCHITECTS

George Wittenberg and Lawson Delony were friends from early childhood. Both developed an early interest in architecture, influenced by the excellent work of Little Rock architects of the period—George Mann, Charles Thompson, and Thomas Harding Sr. They worked (usually for no pay) for local architects after school and during summer vacation.

After high school, both young men enrolled in the School of Architecture at the University of Illinois. Their choice was influenced by Theo Sanders, a rising young Little Rock architect who had graduated from there in 1902. Along with Sanders, they were among the first native-born Little Rock architects to receive a college-level education in architecture. After finishing at Illinois, Wittenberg went to work for an architect in Peoria, Illinois, and Delony went to New York for a year at Columbia and worked part time for the famous architect George B. Post. By 1918, Wittenberg had returned to Little Rock and gone to work as a draftsman for Thomas Harding Sr. By this time, Delony had finished his World War I service, wherein he had been sent to France, and he, too, returned to Little Rock.

In 1919, they formed the firm of Wittenberg and Delony, Architects. The first office was in room 408 in the Southern Trust Building (now Pyramid Place) on the corner of Second and Center Streets. Their description was "two drawing boards, two stools, one waste basket, and no secretary." They had very little

Robinson Auditorium on Markham and Broadway Streets, Little Rock, Arkansas. Constructed in 1939 in the Neoclassical Revival style, it was designed by Wittenberg and Delony, Architects, and E. J. Stern, Architect. Project rendering by George Trapp. *Wittenberg, Delony, and Davidson's archives.*

Original drawing of the First National Bank at Capitol and Broadway Streets, Little Rock, Arkansas. Constructed in 1975 in the Modern Commercial style, it was designed by Wittenberg, Delony, and Davidson, Architects. *Wittenberg, Delony, and Davidson's archives.*

startup money. To produce income, Wittenberg arranged a part-time job teaching mechanical drawing in the mornings and coaching the Little Rock High School football team in the afternoon. Delony manned the office every day, with Wittenberg joining him after his other jobs. All income, whether from office commissions or the school job, was always shared equally—a practice continued for the rest of their professional lives.

For the first few years, Wittenberg and Delony both participated in all the phases of the work: design, working drawings, and construction inspection. As projects multiplied, they divided responsibilities to make better use of their individual talents. They were a good team. Wittenberg was a well-organized, enthusiastic, energetic person who met people easily and worked well with clients. While Delony, too, was an affable, friendly person, he was an extremely talented architectural designer. This led to the general organization that would last through much of their practice: Delony worked at design and production while Wittenberg was responsible for administration and marketing and usually took care of construction inspection.

Initially, commissions were scarce, but the young architects had opportunities to do projects that built their business over time. In 1926, Wittenberg and Delony's first major project came when they were selected as one of the architectural firms for the now famous Little Rock High School. This large project to house two thousand students would be one of the largest high schools in the

George Wittenberg and Lawson Deloney in their first office in room 408 of the Pyramid Building at Second and Center Streets, Little Rock, Arkansas, in 1919. *Wittenberg, Delony, and Davidson's archives.*

United States. The association of architects included Wittenberg and Delony, Mann and Stern, and John Parks Almand. The finished project was a huge success and widely recognized for its overall design and function; it was described as "the most beautiful high school in America."

When the Great Depression hit, the effect on Wittenberg and Delony, as on many, was devastating. Suddenly there was absolutely no work and no income. As he had done to start the firm, now to survive, Wittenberg found part-time work, this time selling commercial heating furnaces but also working at the office on Depression-type government projects designed to help architects and draftsmen. Delony opened the office every day and worked full time on those projects. Delony was appointed head of the Historic American Building Survey for Arkansas. This project paid architects and draftsmen one dollar per hour to measure, draw plans, and write a short summary of historic buildings in the state. This resulted in a valuable collection of plans and drawings of some of Arkansas's most historic buildings, a collection still in use as a reference.

Toward the end of the Depression, Wittenberg was appointed the first head architect for the state of Arkansas in the Federal Housing Administration. The pay was $500.00 a month—a huge amount in those days. As the Depression eased, things began to improve. The main source of work was from the federal agencies created by Franklin Delano Roosevelt's New Deal administration. These agencies—Public Works Administration (PWA), Works Progress Action (WPA), and such—provided funds for a vast array of projects to stimulate the economy of the nation.

In fact, the opportunity provided to Wittenberg and Delony by the federal programs led to the design of college campuses and college buildings around the state, and the firm began to develop a large statewide practice. Some of their early campus clients were Hendrix College in Conway, Arkansas State Teachers College (now the University of Central Arkansas) in Conway, Henderson College (now Henderson State) in Arkadelphia, Magnolia A and M College (now Southern Arkansas University), and Monticello A and M (now University of Arkansas, Monticello). Through all these projects, the firm created associations and relationships that led to extensive work throughout Arkansas.

After the Depression, the firm was also quite busy in Little Rock. One of the most prominent projects was Robinson Auditorium (1940), designed by Wittenberg and Delony and Gene Stern. Other work included the State Health Building on the Capitol Mall, Dunbar High School, and a number of schools for the Pulaski County School District. The firm also designed a number of residences for Little Rock families, including the Frankes, the Bellingraths, the Browns, the Stiffts, and the Kempners.

During the years of World War II, much of the work of Wittenberg and Delony had been for the military. This work generally consisted of housing at

Lawson Delony. *Wittenberg, Delony, and Davidson's archives.*

George Wittenberg. *Wittenberg, Delony, and Davidson's archives.*

Julian Davidson. *Courtesy of William Allen Family Archives.*

training bases and defense or ordnance plants. Wittenberg and Delony were too old to serve, but Julian B. Davidson, employed at the firm since the late 1920s, left to help the war effort. After his return, Davidson was made a full partner in 1946 and the firm name became Wittenberg, Delony, and Davidson.

JULIAN B. DAVIDSON

Julian Davidson was born in 1906 and grew up in Little Rock. While in high school, he worked for the Wittenberg and Delony firm during summer vacations. Davidson went on to attend and graduate from the Architecture School at Washington University in 1928. He graduated first in his class and won the American Institute of Architects Student Medal. He then came to work full time with Wittenberg and Delony. In 1933, he married Irene Davis McCall, and they had one son, Randall.

Davidson remained with the firm through all his professional life, retiring in 1972. He was the first architect in Arkansas to become both a registered architect and a registered engineer. He held Arkansas Architects License #65 and Arkansas Engineers License #509. His later years were spent with his hobby, building model trains. He designed, built, lighted, and landscaped a 480-square-foot O-gauge layout. Appropriately, his house was at the end of Battery Street, overlooking Union Station and the main tracks of the Union Railroad. Davidson died at ninety-one in 1997.

The firm Wittenberg, Delony, and Davidson was involved in the design of buildings that would house many of the office headquarters and the services of the growing city of Little Rock. For example, the headquarters of Arkansas Power and Light, Arkansas Louisiana Gas Company, Blue Cross/Blue Shield, the Arkansas Farm Bureau, First National Bank (now Regions), and the Little Rock Convention Center were designed by the firm. The later Stephens Building, the Peabody Hotel, and phase 1 of the Little Rock Convention Center were designed by Wittenberg, Delony, and Davidson in association with other architects.

Two other facilities stand out in the history of the firm. In 1963, the Arkansas State Hospital retained the firm to design a new mental hospital to replace the antiquated "insane asylum" constructed in the mid-1850s. The architects collaborated with Dr. George Jackson and his staff to incorporate the latest techniques in treating mental patients with the design of the space and environment. The new facility won a number of awards and was visited by medical staff from around the country as well as doctors from England, France, and Germany.

The deplorable conditions in the Arkansas Prison System and national publicity on these conditions spurred the Arkansas legislature to provide funds for a new modern correctional facility. The firm was hired in 1970 to develop a master plan and design the new buildings. Again, the architects were able to collaborate with staff to develop a facility that was designed to accommodate the needs and requirements of a modern prison. And again, the complex won a number of awards, and Tucker and Cummins prisons were visited by prison staff from around the country.

When George Wittenberg died in 1953, his son Gordon became a partner in the firm. And, although Julian Davidson retired in 1972, the firm retained the name Wittenberg, Delony, and Davidson, as it does today. However, leadership in the firm passed from George Wittenberg to Gordon Wittenberg, to Thomas Gray, then to today's president, Tom Adams.

Frank Ginocchio

FRANK GINOCCHIO FIRST APPEARED in the "architectural" record in 1905, working during his teenage years for prominent Little Rock architect Frank Gibb. He was next sighted working as a draftsman for another well-known Little Rock architect, Charles Thompson. In 1906, he decided he wanted to be an architect and left Thompson to pursue a formal education in architecture at the University of Illinois.

After completing his degree, he returned to Thompson's firm in 1910 and was assigned to the supervising staff at the new Arkansas State Capitol. (Charles Thompson was a member of the Capitol Commission and appears to have had some supervisory role.) He stayed with Thompson's firm until World War I. Recognized as a serious and talented young architect, at the outbreak of the war, Ginocchio was made a captain and placed in the Corps of Engineers under the direction of Col. John R. Fordyce of Little Rock. During the war, Ginocchio was architect in charge of construction at Camp Pike (now Camp Robinson) in North Little Rock and Jefferson Barracks in St. Louis.

When Ginocchio returned to the private sector in Little Rock after the war, he found that Thomas Harding Sr. had become a partner in Thompson's firm, a position he had hoped to attain. So he did what a lot of young architects have done—he started his own firm, jointly with his friend Theo Sanders. The two men had been fellow draftsmen. As Sanders and Ginocchio, they made a strong combination; Sanders was the stronger designer, while Ginocchio's wartime experience gave him broad field experience. Like other architects of the period, they made use of the variety of revival styles of the era. During those years, Ginocchio married Bess Rogoski, and they had two daughters, Elizabeth Ginocchio Hoeltzel and Wanda Ginocchio Paganelli.

Frank Ginocchio. *Quapaw Quarter Association Records, MSS 06–15, Butler Center for Arkansas Studies, Arkansas Studies Institute.*

Sanders and Ginocchio continued until 1927. The Thompson and Harding firm had been dissolved in 1925. Thompson, perhaps recognizing the need for younger men to carry on, invited the two to join him as Thompson, Sanders, and Ginocchio. The early years of this firm were severely affected by the Great Depression, and the firm survived mainly on commissions for the design of residences to remodel or make additions to. A few commercial projects were done. Ginocchio called these "the years of austerity."

By the late 1930s, the nation was beginning to pull out of the Depression, and there began to be enough work for architects to be busy again, but Thompson retired in 1938, followed by Sanders in 1941. But for the previous two decades, the firms with which Frank Ginocchio was associated produced some of the major landmark buildings in Little Rock and in Arkansas. In Little Rock alone, these include the Hall Building, Union Bank, Pfeifer Department Store, Forest Park School, Pulaski Heights Junior High, the Ada Thompson Home, and the Little Rock Boys Club, as well as numerous residences.

With Sanders's retirement, Ginocchio was the senior partner, and he offered a partnership to Thompson's son-in-law, Ed Cromwell, who was at the time working for Wittenberg and Delony. Incidentally, as with Thomas Harding's architectural family, the offer of a partnership to Cromwell launched a four-generation family connection with the profession. First there was Charles Thompson and his son-in-law Ed Cromwell. Later, Eugene P. Levy, at the time Cromwell's son-in-law, joined the firm, as did his son Edwin Levy, Ed Cromwell's grandson.

The new firm was called Ginocchio and Cromwell. However, the year of its formation, 1941,

Hall Building at Capitol Avenue and Louisiana Street, Little Rock, Arkansas. Constructed in 1924 in the Classical Revival style, it was designed by Sanders and Ginocchio, Architects. *Photograph by T. S. Gordon.*

Forest Park School at N. Tyler and P Streets, Little Rock, Arkansas. Constructed in 1923 in the Collegiate Gothic style, it was designed by Sanders and Ginocchio, Architects. *Photograph by Gordon Wittenberg.*

also saw the bombing of Pearl Harbor, and plans for the new firm changed drastically. The architects became totally involved in the war effort, with every project having an urgent deadline. To handle this work, they associated with other architectural firms and set up a special projects joint office in the *Arkansas Gazette* Building. Ginocchio was again involved at Camp Robinson designing projects for the military during the war.

After the war, when architectural firms were getting back to normal, Ginocchio, Cromwell, and Associates would go forward and not only would become one of the leading firms in Little Rock and Arkansas but also would grow into international work and for a long time be the largest firm in Arkansas. Through his several associations—with Frank Gibb, with Theo Sanders, with Charles Thompson, and then with Cromwell and Levy—Frank Ginocchio was a bridge between old and new, connecting the generation of architects whose major work was accomplished before World War II with those who followed.

Ginocchio was one of the founders of the Little Rock Club, had been president of the Boathouse Club, and was a member of the Country Club of Little Rock. He was a president of the State Board of Architects and was also the Italian consul's agent in Arkansas, an honorary, unpaid position. He died in 1969 at the age of eighty-three.

H. Ray Burks

RAY BURKS WAS BORN in 1890 in Monticello, Arkansas, and educated in the Monticello public schools. He attended college and studied architecture at the St. Louis School of Fine Arts at Washington University. His early training in architecture began in Monticello in 1915 working for W. A. Halley, Architects.

In 1917, he moved to Little Rock and began working for James H. Bliss, Architect, in that year. During the later part of World War I, he worked at

Dr. Vinsonhaler (left), dean of the University of Arkansas Medical School, and H. Ray Burks (right) at the dedication of a new building in MacArthur Park in 1935. *Courtesy of the University of Arkansas for Medical Sciences at Little Rock Archives.*

Museum of Fine Arts in MacArthur Park, Little Rock, Arkansas. Constructed in 1935 in the Art Deco style, it was designed by H. Ray Burks, Architect. *Charles Witsell's archives.*

Black and Veach Engineers at Camp Pike (now Camp Robinson). After the war he worked again for Bliss, until he opened his own practice in 1922: H. Ray Burks, Architect. He developed a statewide practice and designed many well-known projects both in Little Rock and throughout the state.

In Little Rock, some of his better-known projects included the University of Arkansas Medical School in MacArthur Park; the original building of the Fine Arts Museum, now the Arkansas Arts Center; one of the early buildings for the Arkansas School for the Blind on Markham Street; the Stebbins and Roberts Company office building and factory; and the original Baptist Hospital.

He was especially noted for his design of a number of residences around the state. In Little Rock, his work included homes for the Gunns, Easts, Pickenses, and Baileys. Statewide, he designed for families like the Fullertons in Warren and the Rushings in El Dorado.

Burks designed courthouses for Drew County, Pope County, and Arkansas County; schools at DeWitt and Fordyce; and the Monticello City Hall. He also worked with the famous Arkansas architect Edward Durrell Stone to design the annex addition and penthouse at the Frederica Hotel on Capitol Avenue in Little Rock (later the Sam Peck, now the Legacy).

In 1945, Burks formed a partnership with Bruce Anderson; they practiced as Burks and Anderson, Architects. The firm's most significant project was War Memorial Stadium in Little Rock. Burks continued in this practice until his death in 1948 at the age of fifty-eight.

University of Arkansas Medical School in MacArthur Park, Little Rock. Constructed in 1935 in the Art Moderne style, it was designed by H. Ray Burks, Architect. *Courtesy of University of Arkansas for Medical Sciences at Little Rock Archives.*

Arkansas School for the Blind, West Markham Street, Little Rock. Built in 1939 in the Colonial Revival style, it was designed by H. Ray Burks, Architect. *Courtesy of Janet Warlick/CameraWork.*

Max F. Mayer

MAX MAYER WAS A TEXAN who came to Arkansas by way of New York, but like most "converts," he was an ardent admirer of this part of the country. Though he lived and practiced architecture in Little Rock less than twenty years, he left a lasting imprint in the structures he designed there.

Mayer was born in San Antonio in 1887, in the three-story Italianate limestone castle that had been home to the Wulff family, whose roots reached back to Altoona, Germany. Max Mayer's grandmother, Paula Olivarri, was descended from one of the original sixteen families sent in 1731 from the Canary Islands by the king of Spain to settle wild San Antonio. The mansion where Mayer spent his childhood years, in San Antonio's historic King William District, is today the headquarters of the San Antonio Conservation Society.

Mayer's education included high school at St. Mary's College from September 1899 to June 1902. He studied at Texas A and M in College Station from September of 1902 to June of 1906. His graduation marked the school's first class of architectural engineering students. Upon graduation, he worked in Cincinnati with architect Harry Lake. Later, he

Original presentation drawing by architect Max Mayer of the Arkansas Territorial Restoration at 200 East Third Street, Little Rock. Restored from 1939 to 1940, the facility is now part of the Historic Arkansas Museum. *Courtesy of the Historic Arkansas Museum Archives.*

studied for two years at the École des Beaux Arts in Paris. He won the prestigious Prix de Rome scholarship and studied also in Italy.

He returned to the United States in 1910 and worked in architectural firms from Portland, Oregon, to New York City and back to the West Coast before arriving in Arkansas in 1914, where he joined the firm of Mann and Stern. During his time with that firm, he participated in the design of the Albert Pike Memorial Temple on Scott Street in Little Rock.

On his application for registration as an architect in Arkansas in 1939, Mayer lists the year 1922 as the year he began his own practice as a principal. His architectural practice was mostly residential, and he was best known for his distinctive residential designs in Little Rock's finest neighborhoods. His work can be seen in the Stifft Station area, in Hillcrest, Prospect Terrace, Edgehill, and the Country Club of Little Rock area. The dozens of houses he designed represent a wide range of sizes, prices, and sites, but they have certain features that make most of them readily recognizable as "Max Mayer houses," often including long roof lines and the use of natural country stone. As one friend noted, "His style had flair and restraint."

Mayer left Arkansas at the onset of the Great Depression and returned to San Antonio. He returned in 1939 at the request of Mrs. Fairfax Loughborough, the guiding force behind the restoration of what was then called the Arkansas Territorial Restoration on Cumberland between Second and Third Streets in Little Rock. The old buildings had been sadly neglected for years and were in a state of rot and decay almost beyond saving. With Mrs. Loughborough's political savvy and Mayer's talent, plans slowly took shape to preserve and restore the essential elements of the historic structures. The complex stands today as one of the most important historic sites in Arkansas—restored by Mayer with vision and dedication to authentic detail for all to see and witness life as lived in Arkansas in the early days.

Bennett House, Little Rock, Arkansas. Constructed in 1924, it was designed by Max Mayer. *Photograph by Gordon Wittenberg.*

Kahn residence, Little Rock, Arkansas. Constructed in 1927, it was designed by Max Mayer, Architect. *Photograph by Gordon Wittenberg.*

Wright House, Little Rock, Arkansas. Constructed in 1941, it was designed by Max Mayer, Architect. *Photograph by Gordon Wittenberg.*

After his return, Mayer remained in Little Rock. He had many friends and was welcome everywhere. He was good-natured, well read, and well traveled. As a bachelor, he was much sought after as an "extra man" back when it was important to a hostess to have a gender-balanced table. He played the violin well and often. He was a talented watercolorist, and it was his custom to paint a watercolor for his clients, often of the house he designed for them.

He lived in a room at 1522 Louisiana and took his meals at Miss Mary Leight's at 1522 Arch Street. His death in 1947 at the age of sixty marked the passing of one of Little Rock's true Bohemians; artistic, debonair, talented, choosing to pursue only that which interested him, he was given to lengthy discourses and enjoyed leisurely conversations. He was a man far more likely to quote Voltaire than the morning newspaper.

Erhart and Eichenbaum, Architects

FRANCIS "FRANK" ERHART

Frank Erhart was born in Hot Springs, Arkansas, in March of 1889, the son of Amand and Jane Pratt Erhart. He attended the University of Pennsylvania; like his future partner, Howard Eichenbaum, he had a professional education in architecture. Erhart and his wife had two daughters, Sister Margaret Erhart of St. Louis, Missouri, and Mrs. John T. Rogers Jr. of Little Rock, as well as four Rogers grandchildren. Margaret was a graduate in architecture and worked for a time with her father's firm before taking holy orders. Erhart died in 1979 at the age of eighty-nine. He was a member of the American Institute of Architects.

HOWARD SAMUEL EICHENBAUM

Howard Eichenbaum was born in Little Rock, Arkansas, in 1904 and was educated in the public schools. He graduated from Washington University, St. Louis, with a BA degree in architecture. Eichenbaum made unusually outstanding contributions to his community and profession. The following is a brief listing of an extensive resume:

After World War II, he was instrumental in starting a chapter of the American Institute of Architects (AIA) in Arkansas and forming the state board for licensing architects; subsequently, he served as president of both bodies.

Frank Erhart, Howard Eichenbaum, and John Rauch (left to right). *From Blass, Chilcote, Carter, Lanford, and Wilcox, Architects,* Fifty Years of Design *(1980).*

Howard Eichenbaum. *Courtesy of the William Allen Family Archives.*

He was the first Arkansan elected to the national AIA Board.

He served as regional director of the AIA and as vice president of the national AIA.

He was the first Arkansan to be elected to the fellowship by the national AIA.

He chaired numerous community boards, including the planning commissions for North Little Rock, Little Rock, and Metroplan.

He achieved the highest Boy Scout award, the Silver Beaver.

He was awarded an alumni citation from Washington University.

He was on the board of directors of two banks and one hospital.

He served on two international design committees.

He served as vice president of Temple B'Nai Israel.

Eichenbaum's professional and community service was remarkable, especially considering that much of it occurred in conjunction with an active architectural practice. Howard Eichenbaum died in February of 1973.

Arkansas Baptist Hospital on I-630, Little Rock. Constructed in 1975 in the Modern style, it was designed by Erhart, Eichenbaum, and Rauch, Architects. *Courtesy of the Arkansas Baptist Hospital Archives.*

ERHART AND EICHENBAUM, ARCHITECTS

Frank Erhart and Howard Eichenbaum were acquaintances as relatively young men. Over their working years together, despite a fifteen-year age gap, the two developed a close bond. After their formal educations, both men began their architectural careers in 1920 as draftsmen in the firm of Mann and Stern. When George Mann and Eugene Stern dissolved their practice in about 1928, Erhart and Eichenbaum chose to continue working for Stern and did so for several more years.

According to a history of the firm written later by Eichenbaum, they approached Stern with the suggestion that they become associates. But for whatever reason, Stern was not interested; the two set out on their own, beginning in January of 1930. Eichenbaum left first, with Erhart staying on to finish a project until February of 1931. Their timing could hardly have been worse, since these years coincided with the onset of the Great Depression. Needless to say, there was no work.

Eichenbaum went to work for the Works Progress Administration (WPA) as state architect. Erhart kept the office doors open. Eichenbaum worked nights and weekends helping Erhart. The two located in a two-room office space on the third floor of the Gem Building, across the street from the *Gazette* Building in Little Rock. They brought furniture from home to make a workable office. The rent was thirty dollars a month, but Saul Harris, who owned the building, had a project for them, and this work took care of the rent. Harris's project gave them a start. It was a shopping center with built-in parking at Kavanaugh and Spruce Streets, covering about a quarter block. Their work continued with a few single- and multi-family residences. Parnell Hall at the Arkansas Deaf Mute Institute was their first large project.

By 1938, work began to pick up and the firm was selected, in association with Haralson and Mott of Fort Smith, to design the new $2 million Arkansas State Tuberculosis Sanatorium at Booneville. This was a very large project, even for a joint venture of firms. Other work began to come in, notably at Baptist Hospital in Little Rock, an association that began thirty years of work for that institution.

During World War II, as has been noted earlier, almost all non-military work stopped. From 1941 to 1946, the Erhart and Eichenbaum firm was part of an association of architects and engineers doing work for military installations and wartime housing. The association also included George Wittenberg and Lawson Delony, H. Ray Burks, Theo Sanders, and McRae and Lefever, Engineers. After the war, each of the architects and engineers went back to their individual practices.

In 1945, Erhart and Eichenbaum added John A. Rauch as a partner, and the firm became Erhart, Eichenbaum, and Rauch, Architects. John Rauch had had his own practice prior to joining the associated group during the war. Rauch had served in World War I and volunteered again in World War II but was refused service because of his age. He had married Stella Irene Schott and they had three daughters. Rauch died at the age of ninety-eight in 1990, and his wife outlived him.

Erhart, Eichenbaum, and Rauch grew to be one of the largest architectural firms in Arkansas. Their work included many prominent landmarks in Little Rock as well as projects throughout the state. The firm's projects included the following impressive works in Little Rock:

Veterans Administration Hospital on Roosevelt Road (joint venture)
Little Rock Baptist Hospital Main Campus
St. Vincent Infirmary
Barton Coliseum
University of Arkansas Medical Center
Horace Mann High School
Justice Building, State of Arkansas
Boy Scouts of America Headquarters
Metropolitan Bank
US Federal Building, Capitol Avenue (a joint venture with Brueggeman, Swaim, and Allen and the Cromwell firm)

Not long after Noland Blass Jr. returned from overseas duty with the US Army Engineers, he became a draftsman at Erhart, Eichenbaum, and Rauch; and when he was made a partner in 1956, his name was added to that of the firm. Edgar Riddick Jr. and Lugean Chilcote became partners as well, but all three appointments lie outside this book's time frame.

University of Arkansas for Medical Sciences on West Markham Street, Little Rock, constructed in 1956 in the International style. It was a joint venture of Erhart, Eichenbaum, and Rauch, Architects, and Edward Durell Stone, Architect. *Courtesy of the UAMS Library Historical Research Center.*

Design drawing of Worthen Bank Building at Capitol Avenue and Louisiana Streets, Little Rock. Designed by Erhart, Eichenbaum, Rauch, and Blass, Architects, it was constructed in 1967 in the Modern style. *From the American Institute of Architects Arkansas Chapter's* Dimensions *3, no. 2 (March/April 1968): 8.*

Arthur N. McAninch

THE *ARKANSAS GAZETTE* of May 8, 1932, indicates that Arthur McAninch began practicing architecture in Little Rock in approximately 1929. At that time his firm was known as Petter and McAninch, a partnership with J. R. or Jack Petter. Petter was an Englishman who had worked for the famous Chicago firm Holabird and Root, Architects. He came to Little Rock around 1924 to work for the Mann and Stern firm when their practice was growing beyond Little Rock. He is credited with working on the design of the Arlington Hotel in Hot Springs, Arkansas, and the Washington-Youree Hotel in Shreveport, Louisiana.

In that 1932 article, the *Gazette* reporter wrote that McAninch had completed arrangements to take over the entire business of Petter and McAninch, the firm now to be called A. N. McAninch, Architect. J. R. Petter, a member of the organization for three years, had withdrawn, and we have not been able to determine where Petter went at that point.

During its three years, however, Petter and McAninch had designed many buildings throughout the state, including the Wright Service Station, the Terry Building, the Arkansas Theater, and the Rightsell School Auditorium, all in Little Rock, and

Arthur N. McAninch. *From John Caylor's* A Century of Witnessing: First Baptist Church, Little Rock, Arkansas, 1858–1965 *(Little Rock, n.d.), 84.*

Hope High School, Arkadelphia High School, and an administration building for Jonesboro A and M College. Also, during the research for this book, a fanciful plan for the Little Rock Airport was found, with Petter and McAninch's title block.

McAninch practiced solo until 1938, when he and Bruce Anderson formed a new partnership—McAninch and Anderson. This association lasted until 1941. (Additional information on these years appears in the chapter on Bruce Anderson.) After the war, he joined in one more partnership, McAninch and Mahnker, in 1945. John Roscoe Mahnker Jr. was from Oklahoma, born there in 1909. He was educated at the University of Oklahoma and Arkansas Tech. This firm designed a number of projects in Little Rock and many around the state.

McAninch's most prominent project in Little Rock was the First Baptist Church at Twelfth and Louisiana Streets, constructed in 1941; it is a fine example of Gothic Revival design. He also designed some very fine collegiate Gothic buildings, including five buildings at the college in Monticello (now the University of Arkansas, Monticello). His designs of the courthouse at Hope and the Eudora City Hall were well recognized. He also designed Caraway Hall at Arkansas Tech in Russellville and the John Brown Watson Memorial Library building at what is now the University of Arkansas at Pine Bluff. Arthur McAninch continued the practice of architecture until his death on March 9, 1965, in Little Rock.

A conceptual drawing of a proposed airport for Little Rock, Arkansas, circa 1930, by Petter and McAninch, Architects. *From the* Southern Architectural and Industrial Arts Exposition Official Catalog, *November 9–16, 1929, Memphis, Tennessee (Atlanta, GA: Press of the Southern Architect and Building News, 1929), 71.*

Rightsell School at Nineteenth and Izard Streets, Little Rock, Arkansas. Constructed in 1906 in the Craftsman style, it was designed by Petter and McAninch, Architects. *Charles Witsell's archives.*

First Baptist Church at Eighth and Louisiana Streets, Little Rock, Arkansas. Constructed in 1941 in the Gothic Revival style, it was designed by Arthur McAninch. *Courtesy of Cindy Momchilov/ CameraWork.*

First Baptist Church Education Building at Eighth and Louisiana Streets, Little Rock, Arkansas. Constructed in 1941 in the Gothic Revival style, it was designed by Arthur McAninch, Architect. *Courtesy of Cindy Momchilov/CameraWork.*

Bruce Anderson

BORN IN NEWPORT, ARKANSAS, in 1907, Bruce Anderson was the son of G. Roy and Amelia Frei Anderson. Amelia Frei was born in Lucerne, Switzerland, and Anderson's father was a Scotsman. Anderson grew up in the Little Rock area and attended Castle Heights Military School in Lebanon, Tennessee. He graduated in architecture from Alabama Polytechnic Institute and won a scholarship to the Harvard Graduate School of Design.

In 1933, he married Helen McClain. They were the parents of a son, Bruce Roy Anderson Jr. Anderson Sr. had begun his professional career in Little Rock in 1929, which, of course, was a bad time, for it was the year of the stock market crash. Anderson was hired as a draftsman by George Wittenberg and Lawson Delony's firm in Little Rock. While at the Wittenberg and Delony firm, Anderson had a number of responsibilities, including site supervisor for the Forrest City High School construction and cost estimator for William Peterson, general contractor. By 1934, he was an architectural designer, working drawings and specifications, and was office manager for architect Arthur N. McAninch from 1934 to 1936.

In 1936, Anderson went to Texas for a year to work for Alfred C. Finn, a Houston architect, but he returned to Little Rock in 1937 to form an architectural partnership, McAninch and Anderson, with Arthur McAninch. This partnership lasted until 1941, and for a time in 1942, Anderson was with Allied Architects, the group of architects doing wartime work from the old *Gazette* Building. During the remaining war years, from the end of 1942 until 1945, Anderson, a US Army captain, served as chief of the Engineering Branch at the Pine Bluff arsenal.

After the war, Anderson returned to Little Rock and formed a three-year partnership with H. Ray Burks, Burks and Anderson. Their major project was the imposing War Memorial Stadium. Other work

Bruce Anderson. *From the American Institute of Architects Arkansas Chapter's* Dimensions *4, no. 3 (May/June 1969).*

by Anderson included Calvary Baptist Church, the Second Baptist Church (the successor building to that designed by Benjamin J. Bartlett in the mid-nineteenth century), and several remodeling projects at the Arkansas State Capitol. Outside Little Rock, he had important repeat clients, including what is now the University of Central Arkansas at Conway, Harding University at Searcy, and Ouachita Baptist University at Arkadelphia. After 1948, Anderson established a solo practice, Bruce R. Anderson, Architect; he retired in 1981.

In addition to his numerous professional accomplishments, Anderson was a highly regarded watercolor painter, although he described himself as a "Sunday" painter. He was a founding member of Mid-Southern Water Colorists and a member of the National Watercolor Society. He served on the board of directors of the Arkansas Festival of Arts. His fourteen paintings of historic buildings in Little Rock's Quapaw Quarter was a wonderful collection, which has now been dispersed. Included were the Old State House, the Terry Mansion, Trapnall Hall, and the Capitol Hotel. His paintings appeared as covers for numerous local and national publications.

Anderson was quite active in his community, serving on the Little Rock Board of Adjustment and the Board of Trustees of Arkansas Children's Hospital, and he was a member of the American Institute of Architects. In addition, he was a member of the Ancient Free and Accepted Masons, the Scimitar Shrine Temple, and the Arkansas Consistory. He was a founding member of Pleasant Valley Country Club and attended Winfield Methodist Church. He died in 1985.

War Memorial Stadium (after extensive remodeling) on West Markham Street, Little Rock, Arkansas. Constructed in 1948 in the Art Deco style, it was designed by Burks and Anderson, Architects. *Courtesy of Cindy Momchilov/CameraWork.*

Second Baptist Church at Eighth and Cumberland Streets, Little Rock, Arkansas. Constructed in 1965 in the Modern style, it was designed by Bruce Anderson, Architect. *Courtesy of Cindy Momchilov/ CameraWork.*

Brueggeman and Swaim, Architects

EDWARD FREDERICK BRUEGGEMAN

E. F. Brueggeman was born in St. Louis, Missouri, on July 8, 1905. He was educated in the public schools of Asheville, North Carolina, graduating from high school there. During his high school years, he worked in the afternoons with D. J. Dreyer, an Asheville architect. Having decided to become an architect himself, Brueggeman took a special course in architectural designing at Washington University in St. Louis.

After completing his work at Washington University, Brueggeman worked for an architectural firm in St. Louis, LaBeaum and Klein. He remained with this firm until 1928. In that year, he moved to Little Rock, where he was employed by Thompson, Sanders, and Ginocchio, Architects, until he opened his own practice in 1932.

Brueggeman married Marion Fulk of Little Rock, daughter of Francis Guy Fulk. They had two daughters: Marion Lynn, born in Little Rock in 1936, and Peggy, born in 1938. Over the years, Brueggeman served his profession as a member of the American Institute of Architects, also serving on its National Committee of Public Information. He was for many years secretary/treasurer of the Arkansas State Board of Architects. He was also on the Committee on Design of the National Council of Architectural Registration Boards. In addition, he was president of the Little Rock Exchange Club and a member of the Little Rock Safety Commission. His family has several handsome watercolors that he painted, one the facade of the Old State House. He died in 1985.

GUY WINFIELD SWAIM JR.

Guy Swaim Jr. was born in Little Rock in 1906. He attended Little Rock public schools through junior high and then Castle Heights Military Academy at Lebanon, Tennessee. He graduated from Alabama Polytechnic Institute with a Bachelor's of Architecture. At college, he won the Sophomore Design Competition in 1927 and top prize for his senior thesis in architectural design in 1932. During summer vacations, he worked in John Parks Almand's office from 1926 through 1929, for the Petter and McAninch firm in 1931, and for the Thompson, Sanders, and Ginocchio firm in 1932.

Swaim began his architectural practice in 1933 as a partner with E. F. Brueggeman. He married Mildred Elizabeth Cox at Florala, Alabama, in 1934. Like the Brueggemans, they had two daughters: Sylvia Jewell, born in Little Rock in 1939, and Cecilia Mildred, born in 1942.

He was an active member and a president of the Arkansas Chapter of the American Institute of Architects. He was much involved in the community. A member of the First Methodist Church of North Little Rock, he also served as a trustee there. He was president of the North Little Rock Chamber of Commerce and a member of the Elks Club, Lions Club International, the Pulaski County Planning Commission, and the board of directors of the

E. F. Brueggeman. *Courtesy of the Brueggeman Family Collection.*

Guy W. Swaim Jr. *Courtesy of the Swaim Family Archives.*

William S. Allen. *Courtesy of the Allen Family Archives.*

James C. Wellborn. *Courtesy of the Wellborn Family.*

American Red Cross. Swaim retired from practice in 1974, some ten years before his death in 1984.

WILLIAM SAMUEL ALLEN

Bill Allen attended Little Rock College, earning a bachelors degree in 1927 and a master's degree in 1929. He began working for Sanders and Ginocchio, Architects, and continued there when the firm became Thompson, Sanders, and Ginocchio; he was employed with this firm for fourteen years, from 1922 to 1936. In 1936, he became a partner in the firm of Brueggeman, Swaim, and Allen.

After World War II, Bill Allen became a lieutenant colonel in the US Marine Corps Reserve. His professional service included presidency of the Arkansas Chapter of the American Institute of Architects, and he sat on the Capitol Grounds Extension Committee and the Little Rock Building Code Appeals Board. He was a board member for the National Conference of Christians and Jews and a member of the Country Club of Little Rock, the Little Rock Club, Little Rock Council 812 of the Knights of Columbus, and Our Lady of Holy Souls Roman Catholic Church. One of his favorite projects of the many he worked on was the church and residence for the discalced Carmelite nuns, Carmel of St. Teresa, on West Thirty-Second Street in Little Rock, where it can be seen today.

BRUEGGEMAN AND SWAIM, ARCHITECTS

This firm began with the partnership of E. F. Brueggeman and Guy Swaim (Brueggeman and Swaim, Architects) in 1933 and only three years later became Brueggeman, Swaim, and Allen with the addition of Bill Allen in 1936. They designed a number of landmark buildings in Little Rock and throughout the state. Some of their Little Rock projects include the following:

St. Vincent Infirmary on West Markham Street, Little Rock, Arkansas. Constructed in 1950 in the International style, it was a joint venture of Brueggeman, Swaim, and Allen, Architects, and Erhart, Eichenbaum, and Rauch, Architects. *Courtesy of the St. Vincent Infirmary Archives, Little Rock.*

Front Gate, Mount Holly Cemetery
Veterans Administration Building, Roosevelt Road (in association with Erhart, Eichenbaum, and Rauch, Architects)
Federal Building, Capitol Avenue (joint venture with Erhart, Eichenbaum, and Rauch and Ed Cromwell's firm)
St. Vincent Infirmary (in association with Erhart, Eichenbaum, and Rauch)
Our Lady of Holy Souls Catholic Church
Catholic High School
Pulaski Heights Methodist Church
Arkansas State Game and Fish Commission Building
Arkansas State Welfare Building

In 1953, Brueggeman left the firm to open a solo practice. James Clay Wellborn moved to Little Rock from Texas in 1954 and became an associate with the firm, now called Swaim and Allen. In 1959 he was made a partner, and the firm name became Swaim, Allen, and Wellborn.

Federal office building at Capitol Avenue and Arch Street, Little Rock, Arkansas, constructed in 1961 in the International style. It was a joint venture of Brueggeman, Swaim, and Allen, Architects, and Ginocchio, Cromwell, and Associates, Architects. *Courtesy of the Wellborn Family.*

Veterans Administration Hospital on East Roosevelt Road, Little Rock, Arkansas. Constructed in 1948 in the International style, it was a joint venture of Brueggeman, Swaim, and Allen, Architects, and Erhart, Eichenbaum, and Rauch, Architects. *Courtesy of the Wellborn Family.*

Edwin Cromwell

ED CROMWELL WAS BORN in Manila, the Philippines, in 1909. His father, a collector of revenues for the islands, died when Ed was just two years old. After that, the family moved to West Point, Mississippi. From there, he went to prep school in Pennsylvania and then to Princeton University.

With unfortunate timing, Cromwell graduated with a degree in architecture in 1931, in the early years of the Great Depression. In order to make a living, he did everything from cleaning bricks to moonlighting in established architectural firms. In 1934 he taught high school math. After a short employment with the census bureau in Washington, he was encouraged by friends to take a position with the Resettlement Administration in Little Rock. He moved in December of 1935. He later wrote that he fell in love with the city.

From 1936 to 1941, Cromwell practiced architecture with George Wittenberg and Lawson Delony. During this period, he married Henrietta "Retta" Thompson, daughter of well-known Arkansas architect Charles Thompson. They had three daughters, Trudie, Mildred, and Patricia.

By the early 1940s, both Charles Thompson and Theo Sanders had retired from the firm of Thompson, Sanders, and Ginocchio, and Frank Ginocchio had assumed senior partner status. He offered Cromwell a full partnership position. At Ginocchio and Cromwell, Cromwell assumed responsibility for inside work: design, drafting, and business development. Ginocchio was responsible for construction-phase services. But this was 1941, and with the bombing of Pearl Harbor, most of the parameters of the architectural business changed dramatically. Frank Ginocchio had good quartermaster connections from World War I, and the firm was called into action fairly quickly. The work was nearly all military—housing encampments, airports, munitions facilities.

Ed Cromwell. *Quapaw Quarter Association Records, MSS 06–15, Butler Center for Arkansas Studies, Arkansas Studies Institute.*

After the war, the practice became more normal, although shortages of materials, particularly steel, concrete, and masonry cement continued to plague the construction industry. Over the years, the firm grew and prospered until it became, for a number of years, the largest in the state. The University of Arkansas at Little Rock (formerly Little Rock University) was an important repeat client. The work there started with a master plan and academic core, in the mid 1950s, and the firm has added many separate buildings there. As with the Wittenberg firm, Ginocchio and Cromwell had excellent client relationships on several campuses. Among them were Philander Smith in Little Rock, the University of Arkansas at Pine Bluff, Mackinac College (Michigan), and the University of Arkansas at Fayetteville.

Two very important public buildings designed for Little Rock were the Little Rock Regional Airport in 1967 and the Arkansas Arts Center in 1959. And although international work was unusual for the firm in the 1960s, they designed the staff housing and consul general's residence in Madras, India, in 1965.

An important project for the firm was the home of Winthrop Rockefeller, for whom they designed a mountaintop residence, barn, and several secondary buildings, starting in 1954. In part through Rockefeller, the firm also did quite a lot of industrial work, much of it from the mid-1950s to the early 1970s for firms such as Jacuzzi, Enmar, Timex, Coca-Cola, Orbit Valve, Teletype, Whirlpool, General Electric, Rockwell International, and Johnson and Johnson.

Cromwell was a pioneer in Arkansas historic preservation. His growing interest began with two

University of Arkansas at Little Rock, Main Library on University Avenue. Constructed in the Modern style, it was designed by Cromwell, Truemper, Levy, Parker, and Woodsmall, Architects. *Photograph by Gordon Wittenberg.*

KTHV Channel 11 Building at 720 South Izard Street, Little Rock, Arkansas. Constructed in 1954 in the International style, it was designed by Ginocchio, Cromwell, and Associates, Architects. *Photograph by William Davis.*

historic houses converted to market-rate apartments. Before he was finished, he had rehabilitated seven or eight historic houses, two historic commercial buildings, and the spectacular Capitol Hotel. He chaired the commission of the Arkansas Territorial Restoration (now Historic Arkansas Museum) and worked with most of the preservation advocacy organizations. He was the first Arkansas architect to champion this work in a major way. He mentored several architects interested in this work, including the coauthor of this book, Charles Witsell. In addition, he saw buildings in the larger context of a planner. He helped turn the city of Little Rock back to the river. For example, he wanted to save the old Tennenbaum building as a mixed-use development overlooking the river; although this proposal did not succeed, others did. As his daughter said recently, "He would be so happy to see how wonderful the riverfront development is today."

Cromwell's vision as a planner was not limited to Little Rock's historic areas. He put together a team to redevelop the old ordnance factory into what became Maumelle New Town. Ed Cromwell's active architectural career in Arkansas lasted for forty-eight years, from 1936 to 1984. When he retired, he remained very active in the community as his father-in-law Thompson had done. Cromwell died in 2001.

His large firm had, over the years of Cromwell's leadership, added a number of partners and associates. One of these was Charles Carter, who joined the firm in 1946. A former architect with the Federal Housing Administration, he eventually became a manager of the firm and was its secretary/treasurer as well. Another was Dietrich Neyland, who joined the firm in 1950. Cromwell had sought a designer who could incorporate the new International style into the firm's image. Neyland had worked for well-known architect Richard Neutra, whose work provided outstanding examples of postwar design. Neyland came to Little Rock from Shreveport, Louisiana, where he had designed a new school that had attracted much favorable attention.

John Truemper grew up in Helena and Little Rock. As a child, his interest in architecture was sparked by his family's neighbor, Frank Ginocchio. Later, during World War II, Ginocchio invited him to apprentice as a draftsman at the firm. Truemper then completed his professional education at the University of Illinois and began working full-time at the firm in 1950. Robert H. Millett, a one-time draftsman, received his formal training at the Massachusetts Institute of Technology. He had a particular aptitude for industrial building design. Millett overcame a cancer that caused the removal of an arm; using an elaborate drafting machine, he was able to make precise drawings with only one arm. The Ginocchio and Cromwell firm was one of the first architectural firms to bring engineers in house. These hires included Oliver Gatchell in 1955, Bill Woodsmall in 1960, and Ben Dees in 1964.

The firm's successive names reflected the various partnerships that occurred over the years: from Ginocchio, Cromwell, and Associates to Ginocchio, Cromwell, Carter, Dees, and Neyland, to Ginocchio, Cromwell, Carter, and Neyland and, after Frank Ginocchio died, to Cromwell, Neyland, Truemper, Levy, and Woodsmall and later to Cromwell, Neyland, Truemper, Millett, and Gatchell.

The Capital Hotel (artistic rendering of future restoration) at Markham and Louisiana Streets, Little Rock, Arkansas. *Cromwell Architects/Engineers Archives.*

Joseph Yandell Johnson

YANDELL JOHNSON WAS BORN in St. Louis on October 1, 1911. He graduated from a St. Louis high school in 1928 and studied architecture at Washington University in St. Louis, receiving a master's degree in 1934. In 1931, he had married fellow architecture student Mary Pipkin. She, too, was born in 1911 in St. Louis, and she had earned a BS degree in architecture from Washington University.

A student with promise, Johnson won a national design competition as well as the James Harrison Steadman Fellowship to study and travel a year in Europe. He was particularly pleased to be able to see the works of the modern masters, such as Le Corbusier and Walter Gropius. After travel, the Johnsons moved to Jonesboro, where Johnson worked for Elmer Stuck in 1940. A short time later they moved to Little Rock, and Johnson went to work for the Federal Housing Authority. During World War II, he served in the US Navy in the Solomon Islands; he was a photograph interpreter.

After the war, in 1946, the Johnsons established a practice in Little Rock in a remodeled nineteenth-century house at 113 East North Street; they worked together there for over twenty years.

It should be noted that there were very few women practicing architecture in Little Rock prior to 1950. In fact, it is not possible to determine the extent of Pipkin's involvement in the practice, as only Yandell Johnson's name appears in connection with the firm's projects. As noted above, Mary Pipkin was born in St. Louis; her parents were Jesse Enos and Addie Hardisty Pipkin. The Johnsons established the Mary Pipkin and Joseph Yandell Johnson Scholarship at Washington University in Mary's honor. The scholarship continues today.

Johnson had a decently large practice, with the University of Arkansas at Little Rock Archives finding

Yandell and Mary Johnson. *Courtesy of the UALR Archives at the Arkansas Studies Institute.*

guide to his collection indicating some 385 design projects both residential and commercial. At some point in his career, Johnson must have made the effort to organize his large collection of drawings, letters, photographs, and miscellaneous papers according to archival standards, and he created the fifteen-page finding guide now at UALR. Because of this attempt at organization, it is relatively easy to grasp the life and career of Yandell Johnson.

Some of his work was schools, and there were some churches, some commercial buildings, a fire station, and an apartment building. But the majority of his work was in single-family residences. Even with nearly four hundred projects, however, Johnson is best known for one building. This was the National Old Line Insurance Company, built in at least two phases and including the original building plus an addition. The building was controversial for two reasons: first, its location across the lawn from the Arkansas State Capitol partially blocked the view of the capitol. In addition, Johnson's frankly modern design conflicted with the Beaux Arts style of the capitol. This structure now houses state offices and is called "The 501 Building," after its address.

In 1967, the Johnsons closed the business on North Street, and Johnson associated with Ginocchio, Cromwell, Carter, and Neyland, Architects, from 1967 to 1969 and in 1970 with Erhart, Eichenbaum, Rauch, Blass, and Chilcote, Architects, until his retirement in 1978. He had been quite active in the profession and was a past president of the Arkansas Chapter of the American Institute of Architects. After Mary died in 1987, Yandell married Akers Pence in 1990. She died in 1998, Johnson in 2000.

National Old Line Building at Capitol Avenue and Woodlane Street, Little Rock, Arkansas. Constructed in 1954 in the International style, it was designed by Yandell Johnson, Architect. *Courtesy of Cindy Momchilov/CameraWork.*

National Old Line Building in Little Rock, Arkansas, showing an early design drawing by Yandell Johnson. *Courtesy of the UALR Archives at the Arkansas Studies Institute.*

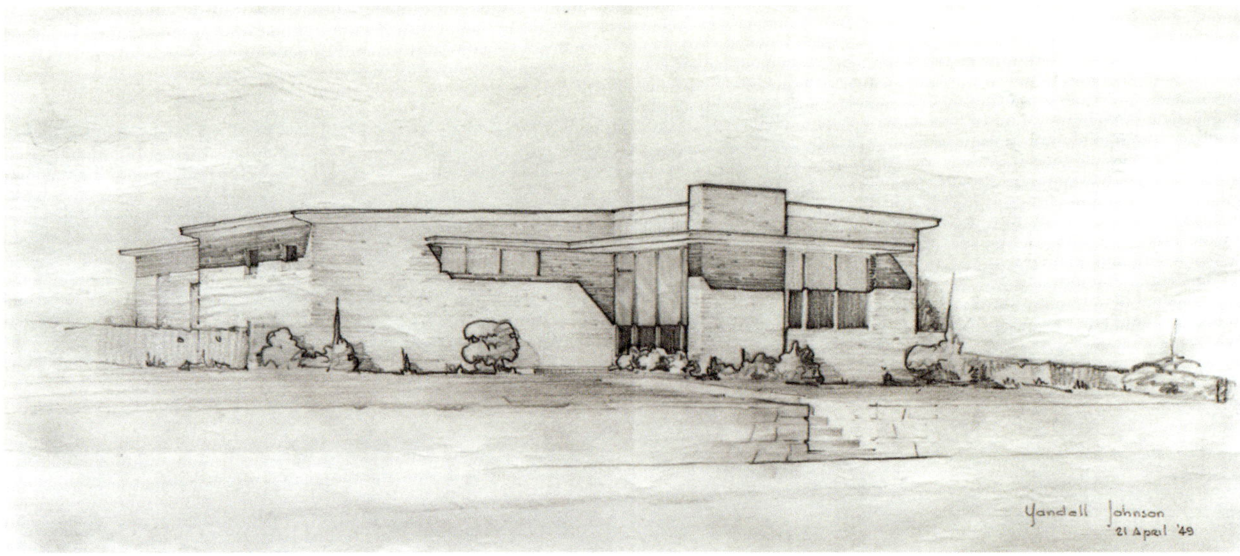

Rogers Wickard Clinic on West Seventh Street across from the Arkansas State Capitol, circa 1950, Little Rock. It was designed by Yandell Johnson, Architect. *Courtesy of the UALR Archives at the Arkansas Studies Institute.*

Trapp and Clippard, Architects

GEORGE FRANCIS TRAPP

George Trapp was born in Chicago on March 20, 1900. He moved to Little Rock in 1914 when his father, Charles Vincent Trapp, took a job with the Big Rock Stone and Material Company as a gravel pit supervisor on Arch Street Pike. The elder Trapp was later employed by the Otis Elevator Company. While Charles Vincent's father was of German ancestry, Trapp's mother, Fannie Rogers Trapp, was Irish. Charles Vincent died in about 1930, and Fannie lived for twenty-seven years more.

George and Linda Trapp. *Courtesy of Wilson Stiles.*

George Trapp continued his early education in the Little Rock public schools, graduating from North Little Rock High School. In 1918 (as soon as he was old enough) he joined the Student Officer's Training Corps at St. John's College, but three months later came Armistice Day and the war was over; he was honorably discharged.

Trapp was interested in drawing from an early age, and one of his instructors was Mark Garver, who co-founded Garver and Garver Engineers. Around 1917, he had begun working for John Parks Almand, a prominent Little Rock architect. Undoubtedly, this early employment influenced his decision to become an architect.

In 1924 he completed a basic curriculum at the University of Arkansas in one year. He then enrolled in Columbia University in New York City to study architecture. Again, he was probably influenced by Almand, a graduate of Columbia. Trapp excelled as a student and was awarded the highly competitive Alumni Award upon graduation. While at Columbia, he won one of the highest awards conferred by the New York–based Beaux Arts Institute of Design for his design and presentation of a synagogue—this in competition with students from Harvard, Yale, and the Massachusetts Institute of Technology. He intended to continue his studies in Paris but lacked

Arkansas State Education Building at the State Capitol Mall, Little Rock. Constructed in 1950 in the Art Moderne style, it was designed by Trapp and Clippard, Architects. *Courtesy of Janet Warlick/ CameraWork.*

the funds. So he went to work for Harvey Wiley Corbett, an architect in New York, to earn the money to study abroad.

In 1927, he went to Paris and enrolled in the prestigious École des Beaux Arts School of Architecture. (Note that this is not the same as the Beaux Arts Institute in New York.) There he met another student from Arkansas, the later famous Edward Durell Stone, who had won a scholarship upon graduation from Harvard. Trapp was an outstanding student and received his Beaux Arts diploma. Many American students were admitted to the Beaux Arts School for further study, but few actually graduated. Trapp did.

He would spend the next three years traveling and sketching in France, Spain, Italy, Germany, Switzerland, and England. His sketches of the monuments of the Classical, Medieval, and Renaissance periods—including Sacre Coeur in Paris, the Alhambra in Spain, Ely Cathedral in England, and Mont St. Michel in France—are superb. Fortunately, they are preserved in Special Collections at the University of Arkansas in Fayetteville. For several years his sketches made up an exhibit that traveled throughout Arkansas, praised and admired by all who saw them.

Early in the 1930s, Trapp returned to New York and worked again in Corbett's office, sharing a drawing table with Edward Stone. The two worked on plans for the 1933 World's Fair in Chicago. In 1934, during the Great Depression, he returned to Arkansas and worked for the Public Works Administration. Leaving the PWA, he worked for a defense plant in Jacksonville and then for the Maumelle Ordnance Plant, where he was chief engineer.

Trapp then went to work for architect Eugene Stern. That was when Stern was associated with George Wittenberg and Lawson Delony on the

Robinson Auditorium project. According to his wife, Linda Trapp, George did "a great deal" of design work for Stern and a partnership document was prepared, but Trapp felt the proposal was not in his favor. Mrs. Trapp quoted her husband as responding that "we" would starve to death before he would sell his talent anymore. With that, he opened his own office. As a designer, Trapp was able to incorporate traditional elements based on classical and medieval styles with clean and streamlined forms associated with modern architecture of the mid-twentieth century.

Around 1947, he formed a partnership with Sam Clippard; the firm was called Trapp and Clippard, Architects.

SAMUEL EBBETT CLIPPARD

Sam Clippard was born in 1907 in Little Rock and grew up there. He attended Little Rock public schools and graduated from Little Rock High School. He entered Washington University in St. Louis, Missouri, to study architecture and graduated in 1929. He married Beatrice Audrian of St. Louis in 1929. They had two daughters, Joyce and Betty. After college, Clippard came home to Arkansas and practiced architecture in Little Rock and El Dorado until World War II. During the war years, he served in the US Navy's Civil Engineering Corps.

After the war, Clippard returned to Arkansas and practiced in El Dorado until 1947, when he moved back to Little Rock and went into partnership with

Pulaski Heights Presbyterian Church at Woodlawn and Walnut Streets, Little Rock, Arkansas. Constructed in 1957 in the Colonial Revival style, it was designed by Trapp and Clippard, Architects. *Courtesy of Janet Warlick/CameraWork.*

George Trapp. In 1963, Clippard retired from the firm, but not to quit working. Rather, this move was to allow him time to follow a dream of many years—the creation of a retirement home for aging people in Little Rock. This project of his became Presbyterian Village. Clippard had studied the problems of housing the elderly for many years, and in 1962 he persuaded his fellow Presbyterians to establish a steering committee to explore his idea. He gave a five and a half acre tract of land that he owned in west Little Rock to become the site of the proposed building. Using his training and experience in architecture as well as his studies of the aging, he designed one of the first such facilities in Arkansas. He supervised the construction of Presbyterian Village and served as its first administrator from its opening in 1965 until his retirement from this position in 1977.

Clippard had always been a good citizen of his community and his church. He was an active Rotarian. He served on the board and later as president of Goodwill Industries. He was very active at Pulaski Heights Presbyterian Church and led Boy Scout Troop 21 for many years.

TRAPP AND CLIPPARD, ARCHITECTS

From its formation, the firm of Trapp and Clippard was successful and designed a number of important projects in Little Rock and around the state. In 1954, Hal Phelps was made a partner of the firm and its name became Trapp, Clippard, and Phelps, Architects. As seen above, Clippard retired in 1963 to work on Presbyterian Village, and the practice continued as Trapp and Phelps until Trapp's retirement in 1966. Some of the major projects by Trapp, by Trapp and Clippard, or by Trapp, Clippard, and Phelps include the following (all except the chapel at Petit Jean are located in Little Rock):

State Education Building, Capitol Mall
State Forestry Building, Roosevelt Road
Pulaski Heights Presbyterian Church
Baptist Hospital Medical Arts Building
Hall High School (in association with others)
Gibbs Elementary School
Walton residence, Walton Heights
Padberg residence, Palisades Drive
Chapel of the Transfiguration, Camp Mitchell, Petit Jean Mountain
Witt Stephens House, Palisades Drive
Frank Bauer residence

The firm undertook several projects outside Little Rock; one of these was Westminster Presbyterian Church in Hot Springs. Trapp died in 1980, Clippard in 1998.

APPENDIX 1

LISTED ARCHITECTS IN LITTLE ROCK, 1833–1950

The following is a master list of those who called themselves architects in Little Rock during the period 1833 to 1950. The names in boldface are those whose biographies are included in this book. The year beside each name is the first year each appeared in a Little Rock listing or is known to have worked here. There are slight discrepancies between some city directory dates and dates given in other sources because of the necessary time delay between each architect's handing in his information and the availability of the printed directory.

1834 **George Weigart**
1840 Henry F. Pendelton
1844 **R. Larrimore**
1845 **Malacha Abbott**
1859 J. H. Smith
1859 **P. C. Spaulding**
1867 Charles C. Ordman
1869 Samuel McCormick
1870 Milton Haney
1870 George C. Price
1870 **Arnold Syberg**
1870 Charles E. Webb
1871 **John D. Edwards**
1871 **Henry C. Green Sr.**
1871 **H. C. Green Jr.**
1877 **Thomas Harding I**
1878 Robert P. Thornton
1880 **Ambrose Pettefer**
1880 **Harry Pettefer**
1881 **Alexander M. Bailey**
1881 D. W. Gaskill
1883 John H. Wood
1886 **Benjamin J. Bartlett**
1886 **Elmo G. Harris**
1886 **Fred J. H. Rickon**
1887 **Casper Kusener Jr.**
1887 Thomas McDermott
1887 **Maxmillian Orlopp Jr.**
1887 Alonzo H. Stillman
1887 A. Wieczorek
1890 **Frank W. Gibb**
1890 William Harter
1890 **Charles L. Thompson**
1893 Augustus L. Breysacher
1893 Eli M. Ford
1893 Thomas L. Ford
1893 David Foucart
1893 Marshall A. Henderson
1895 James W. Gaskill
1901 **George Richard Mann**
1903 J. Eli Blount
1903 Milton A. Hyatt
1906 P. de V. Burton
1906 Aloysius H. Downey
1906 Harry J. Harker
1906 **Theodore M. Sanders**
1908 Samuel M. Fent
1908 Clyde A. Ferrell
1908 Frank W. Hunt
1908 James W. Lasha
1908 James M. Whitehead
1908 Rollie W. Whitehead
1909 Arthur T. Hollingsworth
1909 James S. McClellan
1909 Robert P. Morrison
1909 Patrick Powers
1911 William Dill
1911 William D. Holtzman Jr.

1912 Frank M. Blaisdell
1912 John L. Howard
1913 Herbert H. Newman
1914 Thomas Harding Sr.
1914 Eugene John Stern
1915 Perry Bridges
1915 Harry J. Weston
1916 F. Alexander Dugan
1917 John Parks Almand
1917 James H. Bliss
1919 Lawson L. Delony
1919 Frank Ginocchio
1919 George Hyde Wittenberg
1922 H. Ray Burks
1923 A. L. Matthews
1923 Max F. Mayer
1925 Charles Watts
1926 Nevil C. Withrow
1928 Albert J. Boyd
1928 J. Aubrey Boyd
1928 Milton King (see "George Richard Mann" chapter)
1928 W. E. Parker
1928 Harry Wanger (see "George Richard Mann" chapter)
1930 Howard Samuel Eichenbaum
1930 Francis "Frank" Erhart
1930 Russell Lawrence
1930 Arthur N. McAninch
1930 J. R. Petter
1930 Jack Wiggins
1934 Edward Frederick Brueggeman
1934 Guy Winfield Swaim Jr.
1935 Frank A. Paitchett
1937 William Samuel Allen (see "Brueggeman and Swaim, Architects")
1937 F. W. Hunter
1939 Bruce Anderson
1940 John A. Rauch (see "Erhart and Eichenbaum, Architects")
1942 Edwin Cromwell
1942 Thomas Harding Jr. (see "Thomas Harding I" and "Thomas Harding Sr.")
1947 Julian B. Davidson (see "Wittenberg and Delony, Architects")
1947 Samuel R. Harris
1947 Joseph Yandell Johnson
1947 Morris Smith
1949 George Blumenauer
1949 John R. Mahnker
1949 George Francis Trapp
1949 David F. Weaver
1950 Samuel Ebbett Clippard
1950 Sidney Lee
1950 Daniel F. Stowers

APPENDIX 2

THE DEVELOPMENT OF THE PROFESSIONAL PRACTICE OF ARCHITECTURE

The early history of the architectural profession in Arkansas was typical of the state of the profession throughout the United States in the nineteenth century. A look at early architects in Arkansas reveals that practitioners who called themselves architects also did many other things. For example, consider these ads from early Little Rock business directories:

> 1880: Pettefer Brothers, Architects and Builders (as builders, the firm sometimes bid on other architects' work, as with the Pulaski County Courthouse)
>
> 1881: D. W. Gaskill and Son, Architects and Builders
>
> 1886: Pettefer Brothers, Architects, Builders, and Brick Manufacturers
>
> 1886: Rickon and Harris, Civil and Mining Engineers and Architects
>
> 1886: B. J. Bartlett, Architect and Superintendent of Buildings ("Neat and Tasty Architecture")

This list suggests that the practice of architecture was merely one of several skills available to these multitaskers. In fact, anyone who wanted to call himself an architect could do so. Some who did were in various building trades; others may have trained by working in the offices of architects already in practice. And some were formally trained architects from one or another of the few schools of architecture in existence then.

An early provider of some formal training for European architects was in England, beginning in 1614, in the Office of the Surveyor of the King's Works. For the next two hundred years, it was an important center for training architects. Another early development in this training was the École des Beaux Arts, or Fine Arts School, established in Paris in 1648. This movement aimed to train architects with specialized knowledge gained through very structured study.

The École des Beaux Arts attracted some of the finest early American architects to Paris early in their careers; as they returned to the United States, they established practices that helped shape early American architecture. These architects included Richard Morris Hunt, Henry Hobson Richardson, Charles F. McKim, and Louis Sullivan. This group and successors from their firms would be instrumental in developing the first schools of architecture in the United States: the Massachusetts Institute of Technology (1868), Cornell University (1871), and the University of Illinois (1873).

As Joan Draper has pointed out in *The Architect: Chapters in the History of the Profession*, by 1898 there were nine professional schools of architecture in the United States, with a total enrollment of 384 students. "Yet," she adds, "the 1900 census reported 10,581 persons calling themselves architects." But, as she noted, "anyone could hang out a shingle" because there were no regulations or state licensing laws, although doctors, lawyers, and many other professionals were required to be licensed. However, by the late nineteenth century it was apparent that the requirement of some formal education and the adoption of standards of practice were needed, if only because of changing technology toward the end of the century. It became essential that architects designing new buildings be trained and qualified to meet the health requirements of sanitary sewage systems and devise safety methods to protect lives from fire and other disasters, as well as have a good grasp of structural engineering to deal with the spans, heights, and complexities of the evolving building types.

The need to regulate the health and safety features of a building led to the first law enacted to license the practice of architecture. This was passed in Illinois in 1897. In 1900, as Draper notes, the American Institute of Architects adopted the requirement that all candidates for membership be graduates of an approved school and, in addition, that candidates pass a special institute examination.

In 1921, thirteen architects in Little Rock formed the Arkansas Chapter of the American Institute of Architects, and twenty years later, in 1941, the state of Arkansas created the Arkansas State Board of Architects to license architects to practice. George H. Wittenberg was made president of this board and held Arkansas license #1. As Wittenberg observed at the time, "The new law for licensing architects will take that section of the building trade out of the horse and buggy stage."

Still, the profession was faced with many challenges that came with the postwar world. A particularly important one was the need to address the problem of the licensing requirements of the individual states. The high volume of work in the nation that had been postponed during the war was an all but overwhelming challenge for the architectural profession. Many architectural firms that had previously been local in nature began to practice on a regional and national basis. This required them to be licensed in each individual state where they worked.

The state requirements usually made it necessary that anyone wishing to be approved had to take an examination that could last from two to three days and be personally interviewed by a state board. This proved to be cumbersome and time consuming, and it created unnecessary delays in important work.

The solution to this problem led to one of the most important developments in the process of architects' licensing procedures, the creation of the National Council of Architectural Registration Boards, or NCARB. This group, working with educators from the major architectural schools in the country, developed a standard, nationwide examination system that, upon successful completion, would license an architect to practice anywhere in the United States. One of the major participants in this effort was Ralph Mott, a distinguished architect from Fort Smith, Arkansas. As well as working to see these reforms through, Mott served a term as president of the national organization.

WORKS CONSULTED

Bell, James W. *Little Rock Handbook.* Little Rock: James W. Bell, 1980.

Blass, Chilcote, Carter, Lanford, and Wilcox, Architects. *Fifty Years of Design: Observation on Style, Commemorating the 50th Anniversary of the Architectural Firm of Blass, Chilcote, Carter, Lanford, and Wilcox.* 1980. Promotional book.

Book of Arkansas: Who's Who in Arkansas. Little Rock: *Arkansas Gazette,* 1913. Issued as a book of utility in the daily newspaper office.

Britton, Nancy. *Two Centuries of Methodism in Arkansas, 1800–2000.* Little Rock: August House, 2000.

Browning, Gayle A. B., ed. *They Made a Difference: Arkansas's Free Masons.* Richmond, VA: Macoy Publishing and Masonic Supply Company, 2003.

Cantrell, Ellen Harrell, comp. *The Annals of Christ Church Parish, Little Rock, Arkansas, from A.D. 1839 to A.D. 1899.* Little Rock: Arkansas Democrat Co., 1900.

Caylor, John. *A Century of Witnessing: First Baptist Church, Little Rock, Arkansas, 1858–1965.* Little Rock, n.d.

Cranford, Frances, Nancy McDonough, and Mary Fletcher Worthen. *Recipes in Perpetuity: Timeless Tastes and Tales from Residents and Future Residents of Mount Holly.* Little Rock: Mount Holly Cemetery Association, 2010.

Crawford, Sybil F. *Jubilee: The First 150 Years of Mount Holly Cemetery, Little Rock, Arkansas.* Little Rock: Mount Holly Cemetery Association, 1993.

Crawford, Sybil F., and Mary Fletcher Worthen, comps. *Mount Holly Burial Index, 1843–1993.* Little Rock: August House, 1993. With Supplements 1 (*1993–1997*) and 2 (*1998–2002*).

Diaz, Lakresha. *Oakland—Fraternal Cemeteries: A Brief History and Tour.* 2009. Pamphlet for use at cemetery.

Donaghey, George W. *Autobiography of George W. Donaghey, Governor of Arkansas, 1909–1913.* Benton, AR: L. B. White, 1939.

———. *Building a State Capitol.* Little Rock: Parke-Harper Co., 1937.

Donovan, Timothy P., and Willard B. Gatewood Jr. *The Governors of Arkansas: Essays in Political Biography.* Fayetteville: University of Arkansas Press, 1981.

Draper, Joan. "The École des Beaux Arts and the Architectural Profession in the United States: The Case of John Galen Howard." In *The Architect: Chapters in the History of the Profession,* ed. Spiro Kostov, 209–37, see esp. 214–16. 1977. Reprint, Berkeley: University of California Press, 2000.

Dunaway, L. S. *Jeff Davis, Governor and U.S. Senator, His Life and Speeches.* With personal reminiscences by L. S. Dunaway and introduction by Judge J. V. Bourland. Little Rock: Democrat Printing and Lithograph Co., 1913.

"George R. Mann's Comments on George W. Donaghey's *Building a State Capitol.*" *Arkansas Historical Quarterly 31, no. 2 (Summer 1972):* 134–49. *Appendix.*

Goodrich, Ralph Leland. "Diaries of Ralph Leland Goodrich: 1859–1867." Housed at the Arkansas History Commission and transcribed online at http://woodrichpoems.wordpress.com.

Guide to Little Rock, 1890: The City of Little Rock Guide to the City of Roses for Visitors and Citizens. Little Rock: Tunnah and Pittaro, 1890.

Hamilton, Emelou M. *Little Rock Photo Album of the 1890s.* Little Rock: James W. Bell, 1981.

Hanley, Steven G., and Ray Hanley. *Arkansas Postcard Past, 1800–1925*. Fayetteville: University of Arkansas Press, 1997.

———. *Around Little Rock: A Post Card History*. Charleston, SC: Arcadia Publishing, 1998.

———. *"Wish You Were Here," Arkansas Postcard Past: 1900–1925*. Fayetteville: University of Arkansas Press, 1997.

Hempstead, Fay. *A Pictorial History of Arkansas, Earliest Times to the Year 1890. St. Louis, MO: N. D.* Thompson Publishing Company, 1890.

———. *Reminiscences of Christ Church*. 1924. Pamphlet.

Herndon, Dallas T. *Why Little Rock Was Born*. Little Rock: Central Printing Co., 1933.

Hinkle and Company. *Hinkle and Company: New Book on Building. Cincinnati, OH: Elm Street Publishing Company, 1869. Catalog.*

Historical Commission of the Diocese of Little Rock. *The History of Catholicity in Arkansas, from the Earliest Missionaries Down to the Present Time.* Little Rock: The Guardian, 1925.

Joseph, Laura. Typescript statement now housed in the Quapaw Quarter Association archives at the Butler Center, Arkansas Studies Institute.

Irish, Sharon. *Cass Gilbert, Architect: Modern Traditionalist*. New York: Monacelli Press, 1999.

Latest Views of Little Rock. S. H. Kross Company, 1906. Promotional pamphlet.

Ledbetter, Calvin R., Jr. *Carpenter from Conway: George Washington Donaghey as Governor of Arkansas, 1909–1913*. Fayetteville: University of Arkansas Press, 1993.

Lemaster, Carolyn Gray. *A Corner of the Tapestry: A History of the Jewish Experience in Arkansas, 1820s–1920s*. Fayetteville: University of Arkansas Press, 1994.

Little Rock, Prosperity City. Jungkind Drug and Photo Supply, n.d. Advertising pamphlet.

Little Rock of Today. N.d. Advertising pamphlet.

The Locomotive. New series 13 (1891): 53. Hartford Steam Boiler Inspection and Insurance Company, Hartford, CT.

Mann, George R. Letter written at the request of his grandchildren, to know of his professional activities. October 6, 1932. Typescript. Quapaw Quarter Association archives, now at the Butler Center, Arkansas Studies Institute.

"Mann, George R." *Arkansas and Its People: A History, 1541–1930. Vol. 3* (1930), 214–15. New York: American Historical Society, 1930.

McDonald, Margaret Simms. *White Already to Harvest: The Episcopal Church in Arkansas, 1838–1871*. Sewanee, TN: University Press of Sewanee, 1975.

A New Year's Greeting. Rickon and Thompson, Architects, 1895. Promotional pamphlet.

Orlopp and Kusener. *Rambles in Manufacturing and Commercial Circles of Little Rock*. Memphis, TN: Historical and Descriptive Publishing Company, 1888. See esp. 119–20.

Pope, John. Speech recorded in the *Journals of the Seventh Session of the General Assembly of the Territory of Arkansas*. Little Rock, AR: Charles P. Bertrand, Printer to the Territory, 1832, 195. Cited in F. Hampton Roy Sr. and Charles Witsell Jr., with Cheryl Griffith Nichols. *How We Lived: Little Rock as an American City*. Little Rock: August House, 1984, 47.

Rice, Kathryn Donham. *A History of the First United Methodist Church in Little Rock, Arkansas, 1831–1981*. Little Rock: Parkhurst-Eaton Publishers, 1980.

Richards, Ira Don. *Story of a Rivertown: Little Rock in the Nineteenth Century*. Privately published, 1969.

Rimmer, Martha, Samuel D. Dickinson, Carolyn Y. Little, Harriet Jansma, Carl H. Moneyhon, Michael David Polston, Linda R. Pine, Timothy G. Nutt, Peggy Harris, John Kirk, et al. *Capital County: Historical Studies of Pulaski County, Arkansas*. Little Rock: Pulaski County Historical Society, 2008.

Roy, F. Hampton, and Ralph J. Megna, eds. *Charles L. Thompson and Associates, Arkansas Architects, 1885–1938*. Little Rock: August House, 1982. In cooperation with the Quapaw Quarter Association.

Roy, F. Hampton Sr., and Charles Witsell Jr., with Cheryl Griffith Nichols. *How We Lived: Little Rock as an American City*. Little Rock: August House, 1984.

Rush, Kimberly Reynolds. *Historic Photos of Little Rock*. Nashville, TN: Turner Publishing Company, 2009.

Schmand, Del. *Heritage of First Lutheran Church, Little Rock, Arkansas, 1868–1988*. North Little Rock: Horton Brothers Printing Co., 1988.

Schuette, Shirley, and Nathanial Sawyer. *From Carnegie to Cyberspace: 100 Years at the Central Arkansas Library System*. Little Rock: Butler Center Books, 2010.

Shinn, Josiah H. *Pioneers and Makers of Arkansas*. Little Rock: Genealogical and Historical Publishing Co., 1908.

Souvenir of Little Rock, City of Roses, 1902–1903. N.d. Promotional pamphlet.

The State Geological Surveys of the United States. Bulletin 465. Compiled under the direction of C. W. Hays. Washington, DC: Government Printing Office, 1911. See esp. 18.

Stern, Eugene. Letter to Howard Eichenbaum. April 27, 1939. Quapaw Quarter Association archives, Butler Center, Arkansas Studies Institute.

———. Letter to Edward Brueggeman. December 20, 1952. Quapaw Quarter Association archives, Butler Center, Arkansas Studies Institute.

Truemper, John J., Jr. *A Century of Service, 1885–1985, at the Firm of Cromwell Truemper Levy Parker and Woodsmall*. Little Rock: August House, 1985.

US Navy Special Collections and Archives Division. Letter to an Arkansas genealogist about Max Orloff, May 1, 1997. Quapaw Quarter Association archives, Butler Center, Arkansas Studies Institute.

Views of Little Rock "The City of Roses." 1914. Promotional pamphlet.

Walker, Paulette H., and Alan C. Paulson. *Historic Pulaski County*. Images of America Series. Charleston, SC: Arcadia Publishing, 1999.

Wilson, Dreck Spurlock, ed. *African American Architects: A Biographical Dictionary, 1865–1945*. New York: Routledge, 2004.

Witsell, Evans, and Rasco, Architects. "Construction of 1887 Building." Historic Structure Report: Pulaski County Courthouse, provided to then county judge Bill Beaumont, 1979.

Witsell, Rev. William Postell. *Christ Church, Little Rock, Arkansas, 1839–1947*. Little Rock: Christ Church Vestry, 1950.

Witteman, A. *Little Rock, Arkansas: Indelible Photographs*. New York: 1892.

Wittenberg and Delony, Architects. A promotional pamphlet prepared in 1936, printed but not distributed.

Works Progress Administration. *Arkansas, a Guide to the State*. Compiled by workers in the writer's program of the WPA. New York: Hastings House, 1941.

Worthen, Mary Fletcher. *A History of Trinity, the Cathedral of the Episcopal Diocese of Arkansas: Little Rock, 1884–1995*. Little Rock: August House, 1996.

INDEX